I hope this book becomes your go-to guide as you start learning Microsoft Word and Excel. Whether you want to create well-organized documents, manage spreadsheets with ease, or boost your productivity, this book is here to support you every step of the way.

Think of it as more than just a manual—it's a helpful resource designed to make your work easier, whether for personal use or your career. With Word and Excel, you can achieve so much, and the possibilities are endless.

This book is written with you in mind. Take your time, follow the simple steps, and use the tips to confidently build your skills. You've got this, and I'm here to guide you!

Table of Contents

Part 1: Microsoft Word for Beginners

Chapter 1. Introduction to Microsoft Word

Microsoft Word is a word processing application developed by Microsoft. It is part of the Microsoft Office Suite and is designed to help users create, edit, format, and share text-based documents. Whether it's a simple letter, an academic paper, a professional resume, or a marketing brochure, Word provides tools for a variety of tasks.

Key Features of Microsoft Word:

- **Document Creation**: Write and edit text, insert images, tables, charts, and more.
- **Formatting Tools**: Customize fonts, colors, layouts, and designs for a professional finish.
- **Templates**: Choose from pre-designed templates to save time and effort.
- **Collaboration**: Work on the same document with others in real time via OneDrive.
- **Integration**: Seamlessly integrates with other Microsoft Office applications like Excel and PowerPoint.

Why Use Word?

Microsoft Word is the most widely used word processor in the world, and for good reason. Here are some key benefits:

1. **User-Friendly Interface**: Designed for users of all skill levels.
2. **Customization**: Offers flexibility with extensive formatting options.
3. **Collaboration Features**: Allows for comments, suggestions, and real-time edits.
4. **Compatibility**: Works with various file formats like .docx, .pdf, .txt, and more.
5. **Productivity Tools**: Includes features like spell-check, grammar suggestions, and mail merge.
6. **Versatility**: Ideal for both simple tasks (e.g., typing a note) and complex projects (e.g., publishing a book).

System Requirements and Installation

Before installing Microsoft Word, ensure your system meets the following requirements:

1. **Minimum System Requirements**:
   - Operating System: Windows 10 or macOS (varies by version)
   - Processor: 1.6 GHz or faster
   - RAM: 4 GB or higher
   - Disk Space: At least 4 GB available
   - Display: 1280 x 768 resolution
2. **How to Install Microsoft Word**:
   - Purchase or subscribe to **Microsoft 365** via the official Microsoft website.

- o Download the **Microsoft Office Installer** from your account.
- o Run the installer and follow the on-screen instructions.
- o Once installed, sign in using your Microsoft account.
- o Activate the license to unlock all features.

Pro Tip: Always keep Word updated to access the latest features and security patches.

Overview of the Word Interface

The Microsoft Word interface is designed to be intuitive and user-friendly. Here's an overview of the key components:

1. Ribbon

- The **Ribbon** is the horizontal strip at the top of the screen that contains tabs like **Home**, **Insert**, **Design**, and more.
- Each tab is divided into groups of commands (e.g., Font, Paragraph, Styles).
- You can customize the Ribbon by adding or removing commands to suit your workflow.

2. Quick Access Toolbar

- Located at the top-left corner of the screen, this toolbar provides shortcuts to frequently used commands like **Save**, **Undo**, and **Redo**.

- You can customize it by adding other commands, such as **Print Preview** or **New Document**.

3. Status Bar

- Found at the bottom of the screen, the status bar displays information about the document, such as:
    - Current page and total pages
    - Word count
    - Language and proofing status
- It also includes zoom controls and a button to change the view mode (e.g., Print Layout, Web Layout).

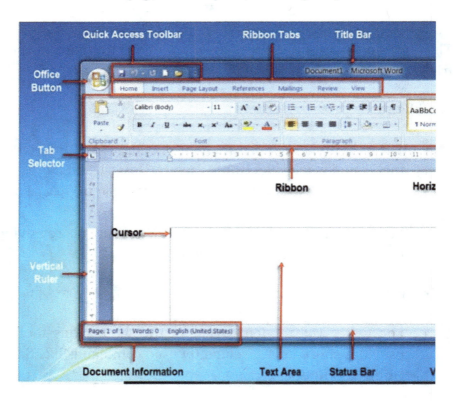

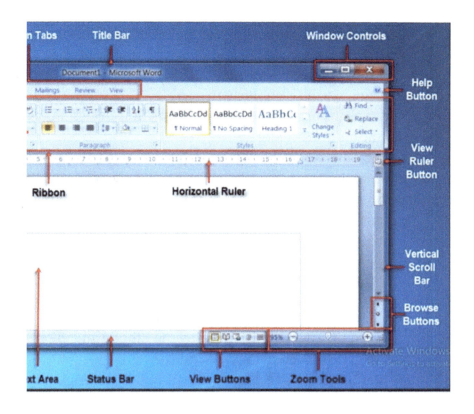

File Menu Overview (Backstage View)

The **File Menu**, also known as the **Backstage View**, is where you manage document-related tasks. To access it, click **File** on the Ribbon. Key options include:

1. **Info**: View document properties, permissions, and version history.
2. **New**: Create a new document from scratch or using a template.

3. **Open**: Open existing documents stored locally or on OneDrive.
4. **Save and Save As**: Save the current document or create a new copy in a different format.
5. **Print**: Set up print options such as printer selection, page orientation, and scaling.
6. **Export**: Convert the document to formats like PDF or XPS.
7. **Share**: Invite others to collaborate or share via email or link.
8. **Options**: Customize Word settings, such as default font, language, and proofing options.

Pro Tips for Beginners

1. **Experiment**: Spend time exploring the Ribbon and different tools to get comfortable with Word.
2. **Use Templates**: Save time by starting with a template for common documents like resumes or letters.
3. **Save Frequently**: Use the shortcut **Ctrl + S** (Windows) or **Cmd + S** (Mac) to save your work regularly.
4. **Utilize Help**: Access Word's built-in Help feature by pressing **F1** or using the search bar in the Ribbon.

Chapter 2. Getting Started with Word

Creating a New Document

Creating a new document in Microsoft Word is simple and quick. Here's how to do it:

1. **From the Start Screen**:
   - o Open Microsoft Word.
   - o On the Start Screen, click **Blank Document** to create a new document.
   - o Alternatively, select a **template** from the available options (e.g., resume, letter, report).
2. **From the File Menu**:
   - o If you're already working on a document, click **File** in the Ribbon.
   - o Select **New** from the left-hand menu.
   - o Choose **Blank Document** or search for a specific template using the search bar.
3. **Shortcut**:
   - o Press **Ctrl + N** (Windows) or **Cmd + N** (Mac) to quickly create a blank document.

Opening, Saving, and Closing Documents

Opening Documents

1. **From Word**:
    o   Click **File > Open**.
    o   Choose from recent documents or browse your computer or OneDrive to locate the file.
2. **Drag and Drop**:
    o   Drag a Word file from your file explorer and drop it into an open Word window.
3. **Shortcut**:
    o   Press **Ctrl + O** (Windows) or **Cmd + O** (Mac) to open a file.

Saving Documents

1. **Save for the First Time**:
    o   Click **File > Save As**.

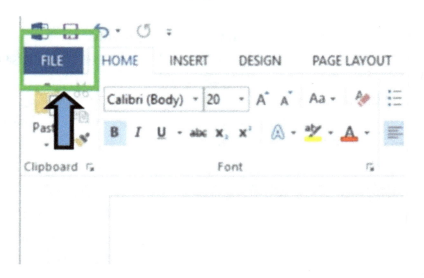

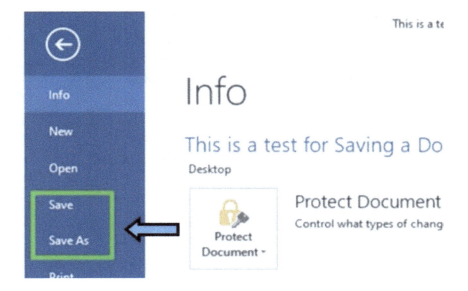

Info

This is a test for Saving a Do

Desktop

Protect Document

Control what types of chang

- o Choose the location to save (e.g., This PC, OneDrive, or a specific folder).
- o Enter a file name and click **Save**.
2. **Saving Changes**:
   - o Click **File > Save**, or use the **Save** icon on the Quick Access Toolbar.
   - o Shortcut: Press **Ctrl + S** (Windows) or **Cmd + S** (Mac).
3. **AutoSave**:
   - o If you're using OneDrive, AutoSave automatically saves your changes in real-time. Ensure it's enabled via the toggle in the top-left corner of Word.

Closing Documents

1. **Close Only the Document**:
   - o Click **File > Close** or press **Ctrl + W** (Windows) or **Cmd + W** (Mac).

2. **Close Word Completely**:
   - Click the **X** in the top-right corner of the Word window (Windows) or the red circle (Mac).
   - Shortcut: Press **Alt + F4** (Windows).

Understanding File Formats (.docx, .dotx, .pdf)

Microsoft Word supports a variety of file formats, each serving a specific purpose.

1. **.docx** (Default Word Format):
   - This is the standard format for Word documents.
   - It supports text, images, tables, and advanced formatting.
   - Compatible with most Word versions and other word processors.
2. **.dotx** (Word Template):
   - Used to create templates with predefined settings, layouts, and styles.
   - Ideal for documents that need consistent formatting (e.g., business letters).
3. **.pdf** (Portable Document Format):
   - Saves the document in a format that's easy to share and view on any device.
   - Preserves formatting and prevents edits unless opened in a PDF editor.
   - To save as a PDF: Click **File** > **Save As**, and choose **PDF** as the file type.

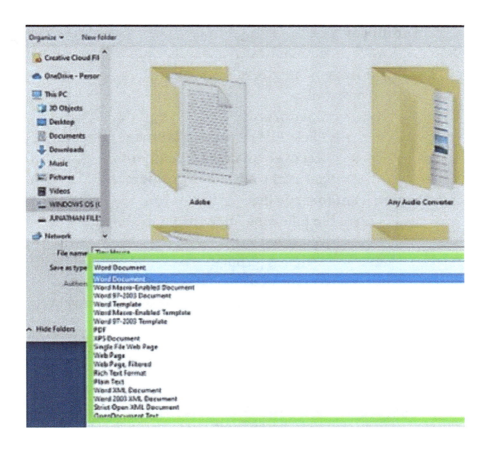

Pro Tip: Use the appropriate file format based on your needs. For example, save a working file as **.docx** but share it as **.pdf** to lock the formatting.

Recovering Unsaved Documents

Losing unsaved work can be stressful, but Microsoft Word has tools to help recover your files.

1. **AutoRecover**:
   - o Word automatically saves backup copies of your document at intervals.
   - o To recover:
     - Open Word.
     - Click **File** > **Info** > **Manage Document** > **Recover Unsaved Documents**.
     - Select the file and click **Open**.
2. **Search Temporary Files**:
   - o Go to the following folder on your computer:
     - **Windows**:
       C:\Users\[YourUsername]\AppData\Local\
       Microsoft\Office\UnsavedFiles
     - **Mac**: Use Finder to search for "AutoRecovery."
3. **Check OneDrive**:
   - o If you've been working on a file saved in OneDrive, log in to your account and check the **Version History** or **Recycle Bin**.
4. **Enable AutoSave and Set Save Intervals**:
   - o Go to **File** > **Options** > **Save**.
   - o Enable **AutoSave** and set the interval for saving to a shorter time (e.g., every 5 minutes).

Pro Tips for Beginners

1. **Organize Your Files**: Create folders to store documents based on categories (e.g., personal, work, projects).
2. **Use OneDrive**: Save files to the cloud for easy access and automatic backups.

3. **Learn Shortcuts**: Familiarize yourself with basic keyboard shortcuts like **Ctrl + S** (Save) and **Ctrl + O** (Open) to save time.
4. **Experiment Safely**: Use temporary documents to practice creating, saving, and opening files without worrying about losing important data.

Chapter 3. Basic Text Editing and Formatting

Typing, Selecting, Copying, Cutting, and Pasting Text

Typing Text

1. Place your cursor where you want to start typing.
   - Click in the blank document or within a paragraph to position the cursor.
2. Begin typing using your keyboard.
   - Use the **Spacebar** to add spaces between words and the **Enter key** to start a new paragraph.

Selecting Text

1. **Using the Mouse**:
   - Click and drag your cursor over the text you want to select.
2. **Using the Keyboard**:
   - Hold **Shift** and use the arrow keys to select text.
3. **Selecting All Text**:
   - Press **Ctrl + A** (Windows) or **Cmd + A** (Mac) to select the entire document.

Copying Text

1. Select the text you want to copy.
2. Press **Ctrl + C** (Windows) or **Cmd + C** (Mac).
    - Alternatively, right-click the selected text and choose **Copy** from the menu.

Cutting Text

1. Select the text you want to cut.
2. Press **Ctrl + X** (Windows) or **Cmd + X** (Mac).
    - Alternatively, right-click the selected text and choose **Cut** from the menu.

Pasting Text

1. Place your cursor where you want to paste the text.
2. Press **Ctrl + V** (Windows) or **Cmd + V** (Mac).
    - Alternatively, right-click and select **Paste** from the menu.
3. **Pasting Options**: After pasting, a small **Paste Options** icon will appear. Click it to choose:
    - **Keep Source Formatting**: Maintains the original formatting.
    - **Merge Formatting**: Matches the formatting of the surrounding text.
    - **Keep Text Only**: Removes all formatting.

Formatting Fonts: Bold, Italics, Underline, and Color

Changing Font Style

1. **Select Text**: Highlight the text you want to format.
2. **Change Font**:
   - Go to the **Home** tab in the Ribbon.
   - Use the **Font dropdown menu** to choose a new font (e.g., Arial, Times New Roman).

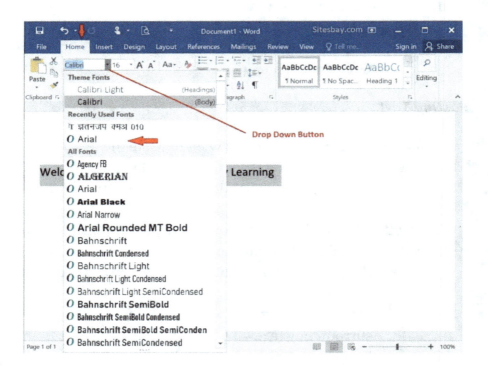

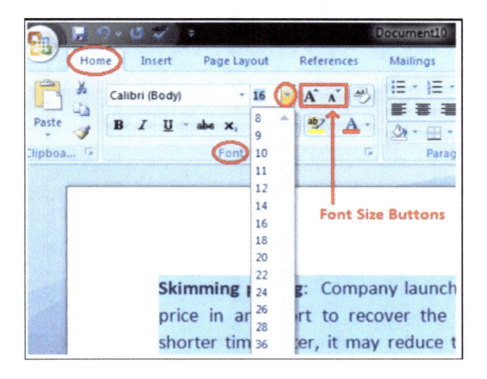

Different ways to change font size

Bold, Italics, and Underline

1. **Bold Text**:
   - o Select the text and click the **B** icon in the Ribbon (Home > Font).
   - o Shortcut: Press **Ctrl + B** (Windows) or **Cmd + B** (Mac).

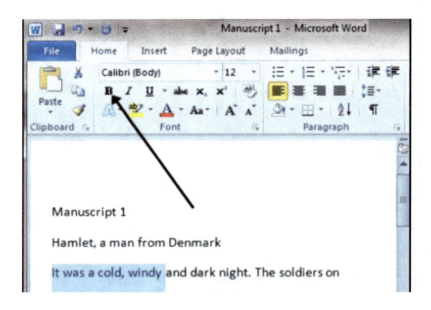

2. **Italicize Text**:
   - Select the text and click the **I** icon.
   - Shortcut: Press **Ctrl + I** (Windows) or **Cmd + I** (Mac).

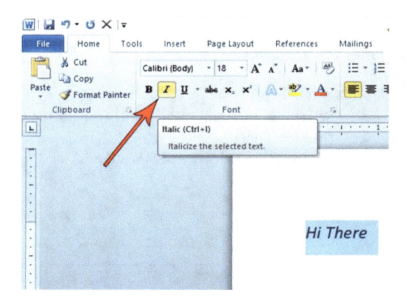

3. **Underline Text**:
   - ○ Select the text and click the **U** icon.
   - ○ Shortcut: Press **Ctrl + U** (Windows) or **Cmd + U** (Mac).

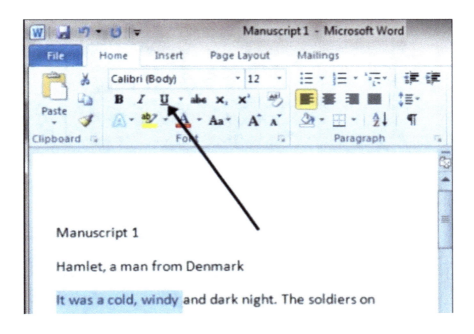

Changing Font Color

1. Highlight the text you want to change.
2. Go to the **Font Color** icon in the Ribbon (Home > Font).
3. Click the dropdown arrow to open the color palette and choose a color.
4. If none of the standard colors suit your needs, select **More Colors** to customize your own.

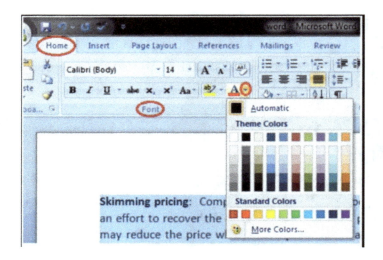

Changing font color

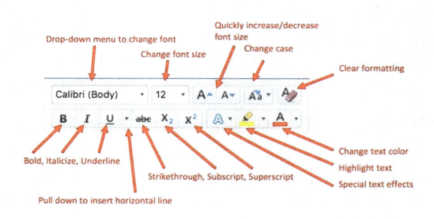

Using the Format Painter Tool

The Format Painter is a powerful tool that copies formatting from one part of the document to another.

Steps to Use the Format Painter

1. **Select the Text with Formatting You Want to Copy**:
   - Highlight the text or paragraph that has the formatting you wish to replicate.
2. **Activate the Format Painter**:
   - Click the **Format Painter** icon in the Ribbon (Home > Clipboard).
   - Your cursor will change to a small paintbrush icon.
3. **Apply the Formatting**:
   - Click and drag over the text or area where you want to apply the copied formatting.

Using Format Painter Multiple Times

1. **Double-Click the Format Painter Icon**:
   - This allows you to apply the formatting to multiple areas without reactivating the tool.
2. **Deactivate the Tool**:
   - Press the **Escape (Esc)** key to turn off the Format Painter.

Pro Tips for Beginners

1. **Practice with Shortcuts**: Familiarize yourself with basic formatting shortcuts like **Ctrl + B** (Bold) to speed up your workflow.
2. **Avoid Overloading Formats**: Use bold, italics, and underline sparingly to keep your document clean and professional.
3. **Experiment Safely**: Create a test document where you can practice formatting and using the Format Painter without fear of ruining important files.

Chapter 4. Paragraph Formatting

Adjusting Line Spacing and Indents

Adjusting Line Spacing

Line spacing refers to the amount of space between lines in a paragraph.

1. **Select the Paragraph**:
   - Highlight the paragraph or block of text you want to adjust.
2. **Open the Line Spacing Menu**:
   - Go to the **Home** tab and locate the **Paragraph group**.
   - Click the **Line and Paragraph Spacing** icon (a set of horizontal lines with arrows).

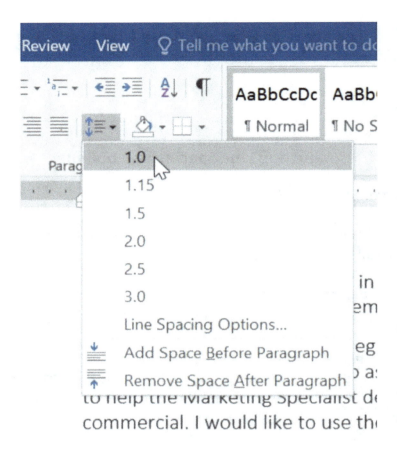

3. **Choose a Spacing Option**:
   o Select from predefined options like **1.0**, **1.5**, **2.0**, etc.
4. **Custom Line Spacing**:
   o Click **Line Spacing Options** at the bottom of the menu.
   o In the dialog box, adjust the **Line Spacing** dropdown (Single, 1.5, Double, etc.).
   o Set the **Before** and **After Spacing** to add space before or after paragraphs.

Setting Indents

Indents control how far text is pushed from the left or right margin.

1. **First Line Indent**:
   - Place your cursor in the paragraph or highlight multiple paragraphs.
   - Drag the **First Line Indent marker** (small triangle) on the ruler to the desired position.
   - Alternatively, go to the **Paragraph group** in the **Home tab**, click the arrow at the bottom-right corner, and set the **Indentation > Special** dropdown to **First Line**.

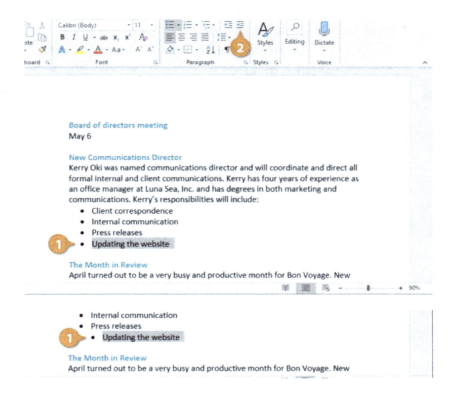

2. **Hanging Indent**:
   - o Use the **Hanging Indent marker** (upside-down triangle) on the ruler.
   - o This is useful for creating bibliographies or outlines.
3. **Left and Right Indents**:
   - o Drag the rectangular markers on the ruler to indent the entire paragraph from the left or right margin.

Setting Paragraph Alignment (Left, Center, Right, Justify)

1. **Select the Paragraph(s)**:
   - o Highlight the paragraph or text block.
2. **Choose an Alignment Option**:
   - o Go to the **Home tab** in the Ribbon and locate the **Paragraph group**.
   - o Select the desired alignment:
     - **Left Align**: Press **Ctrl + L** (Windows) or **Cmd + L** (Mac).
     - **Center Align**: Press **Ctrl + E** (Windows) or **Cmd + E** (Mac).
     - **Right Align**: Press **Ctrl + R** (Windows) or **Cmd + R** (Mac).
     - **Justify**: Press **Ctrl + J** (Windows) or **Cmd + J** (Mac).

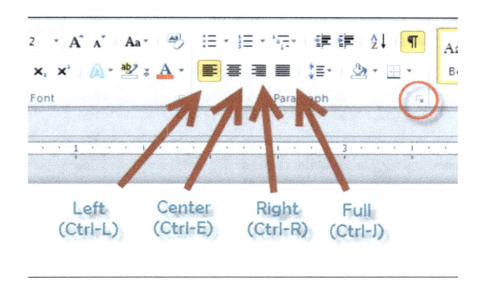

3. **Quick Alignment Shortcut**:
   - Right-click the text, select **Paragraph**, and set alignment in the dialog box.

Creating Bulleted and Numbered Lists

Bulleted Lists

1. **Start a Bulleted List**:
   - Go to the **Home tab** and click the **Bullets** icon in the **Paragraph group**.
2. **Choose a Bullet Style**:
   - Click the dropdown arrow next to the **Bullets** icon to select from predefined symbols.

29

- Choose **Define New Bullet** to use custom symbols, pictures, or fonts.

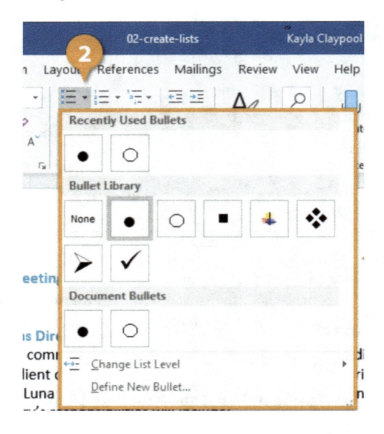

3. **Add Bullets Automatically**:
    - Type - *followed by a space** to instantly start a bulleted list.

Numbered Lists

1. **Start a Numbered List**:
    - Go to the **Home tab** and click the **Numbering** icon.
2. **Choose a Numbering Style**:

- Click the dropdown arrow next to the **Numbering** icon to select number formats (e.g., Roman numerals, letters).
- Use **Define New Number Format** for custom styles.

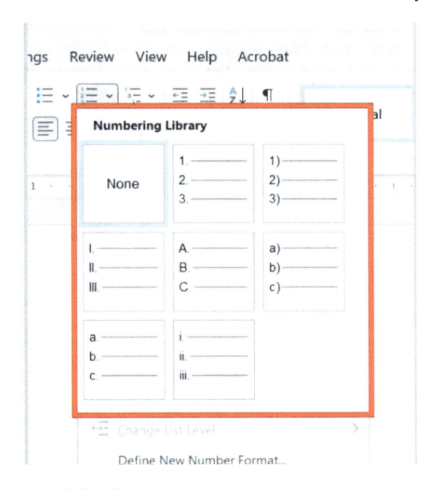

3. **Multilevel Lists**:
  - For sub-items, press **Tab** to create a nested list.

Adding Borders and Shading to Paragraphs

Adding Borders

1. **Select the Paragraph**:
   - Highlight the paragraph or block of text.
2. **Open the Borders Menu**:
   - Go to the **Home tab**, locate the **Paragraph group**, and click the **Borders** icon (a square box).
3. **Choose a Border Option**:
   - Select options like **Bottom Border, Top Border, All Borders**, etc.
4. **Customize Borders**:
   - Click **Borders and Shading** in the dropdown menu.
   - In the dialog box:
     - Choose the **Style, Color**, and **Width** for your border.
     - Apply it to **Text** or **Paragraph**.

Adding Shading

1. **Select the Paragraph**:
   - Highlight the text you want to shade.
2. **Open the Shading Menu**:
   - Go to the **Home tab**, locate the **Paragraph group**, and click the **Shading** icon (paint bucket).
3. **Choose a Color**:
   - Select a color from the palette to apply shading to the background of the text.

Pro Tips for Beginners

1. **Use Ruler Guides**: Turn on the ruler (View tab > Show > Ruler) for precise adjustments to indents and alignment.
2. **Practice Multilevel Lists**: They're invaluable for creating structured documents like outlines or reports.
3. **Experiment with Borders**: Use borders to highlight key paragraphs like headings or summaries.

Chapter 5. Page Layout and Design Basics

Setting Page Margins, Orientation, and Size

Setting Page Margins

Margins define the amount of white space around the edges of your document.

1. **Open the Page Layout Menu**:
   - Go to the **Layout tab** (or **Page Layout** in older versions).
2. **Select Margins**:
   - In the **Page Setup group**, click **Margins**.
3. **Choose a Predefined Margin Setting**:
   - Select from options like **Normal** (1" margins), **Narrow** (0.5" margins), **Wide** (1.5" margins), or **Custom Margins**.

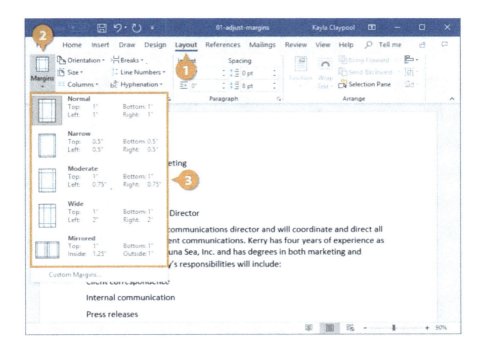

4. **Custom Margins**:
   o To manually adjust margins, click **Custom Margins** at the bottom of the dropdown menu.
   o In the **Page Setup dialog box**, set the **Top**, **Bottom**, **Left**, and **Right** margins as needed.

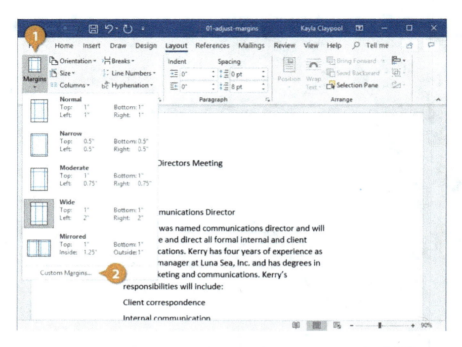

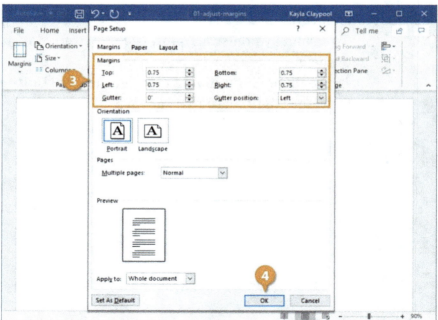

Setting Page Orientation

Page orientation determines the layout of your page—either **Portrait** or **Landscape**.

1. **Change Orientation**:
    o Go to the **Layout tab** and click **Orientation** in the **Page Setup group**.
    o Choose between **Portrait** (vertical) or **Landscape** (horizontal).

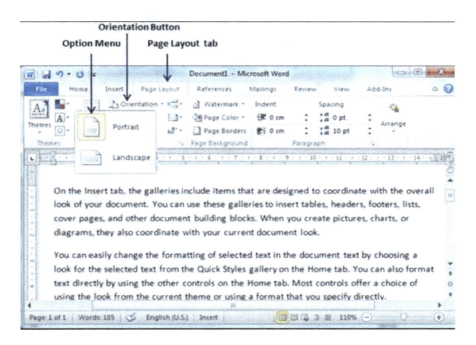

2. **Apply to Specific Sections**:
    o If you want to apply a different orientation to only a section of your document, use **Section Breaks** (see below).

37

Setting Page Size

Page size controls the dimensions of your document.

1. **Change Page Size**:
   o Go to the **Layout tab**, click **Size** in the **Page Setup group**.
   o Choose from standard sizes like **Letter** (8.5" x 11"), **A4**, **Legal**, or click **More Paper Sizes** for custom dimensions.

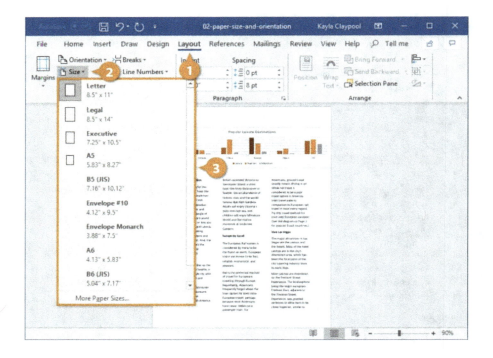

2. **Custom Page Size**:
   o In the **Page Setup dialog box**, under **Paper**, you can manually set the **Width** and **Height** of your page.

Using Page Breaks and Section Breaks

Page Breaks

A **Page Break** creates a new page within your document, automatically pushing content onto the next page.

1. **Insert a Page Break**:
   - Place your cursor where you want the new page to start.
   - Go to the **Insert tab** and click **Page Break** (or use the shortcut **Ctrl + Enter**).

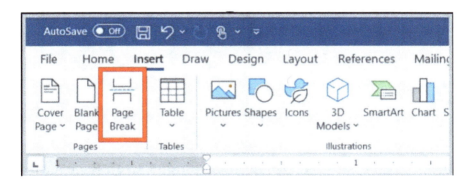

2. **View and Remove Page Breaks**:
   - To see page breaks, turn on **Show/Hide** in the **Home tab** (¶ symbol).
   - To delete a page break, place the cursor directly before the break and press **Delete**.

Section Breaks

A **Section Break** divides your document into distinct sections, allowing for different formatting settings, such as different headers or footers in different parts of the document.

1. **Insert a Section Break**:
   - o Place your cursor where you want the new section to begin.
   - o Go to the **Layout tab** and click **Breaks** in the **Page Setup group**.

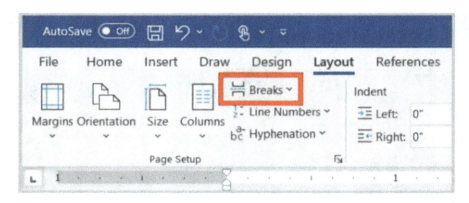

   - o Choose **Next Page**, **Continuous**, **Even Page**, or **Odd Page**.

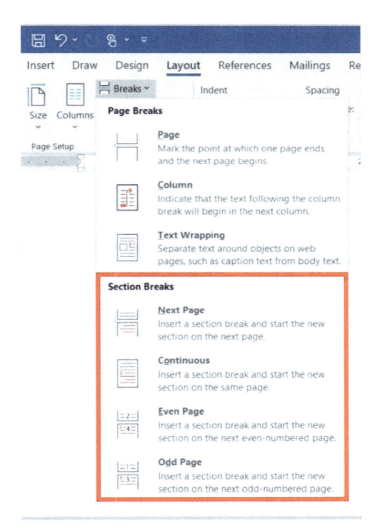

2. **Customize Sections**:
   - After inserting a section break, you can apply different page numbers, margins, orientation, headers, footers, etc., to each section.

Working with Headers, Footers, and Page Numbers

Adding Headers and Footers

Headers and footers appear at the top and bottom of each page, respectively.

1. **Insert a Header or Footer**:
    - Go to the **Insert tab** and click **Header** or **Footer** in the **Header & Footer group**.

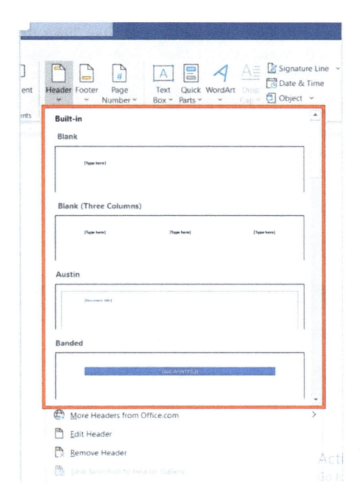

- o Choose a pre-designed style or select **Edit Header** or **Edit Footer** for more control.

2. **Edit the Header or Footer**:
   - o Double-click inside the header or footer area to activate it.
   - o You can add text, images, or even fields like **Date**, **File Name**, or **Page Number**.

3. **Closing the Header/Footer**:

- When you're done editing, click **Close Header and Footer** in the **Header & Footer Tools** tab or simply double-click outside the header/footer area.

Adding Page Numbers

Page numbers can be inserted in headers, footers, or anywhere within your document.

1. **Insert Page Numbers**:
   - Go to the **Insert tab** and click **Page Number** in the **Header & Footer group**.

   - Choose the **Top of Page**, **Bottom of Page**, or **Page Margins** option, then select a style.

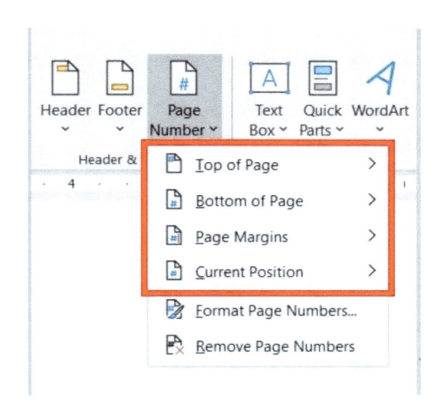

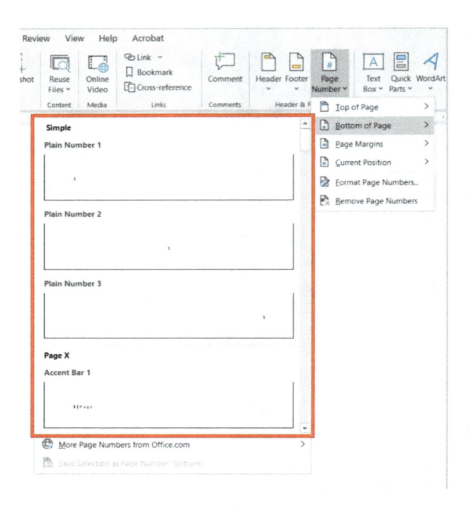

2. **Customize Page Numbers**:

   o To format page numbers, click **Format Page Numbers** from the **Page Number** dropdown menu.

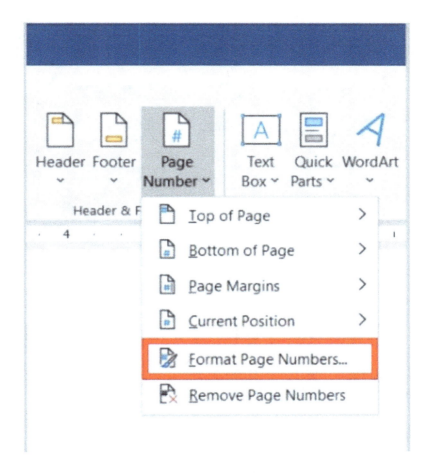

- o You can select the numbering format (1, 2, 3; i, ii, iii; etc.), and choose whether to start numbering from a specific number.

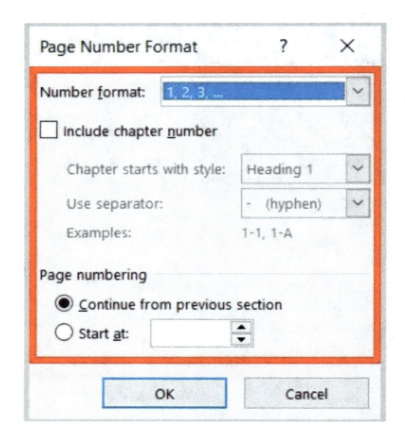

3. **Remove Page Numbers**:
   - ○ To delete page numbers, click **Page Number** in the **Insert tab**, and select **Remove Page Numbers**.

Pro Tips for Beginners

1. **Use Section Breaks to Control Formatting**: If you're working on a large document with different sections, section

breaks will allow you to apply specific formatting (like headers or footers) to different parts of your document.

2. **Page Breaks for Organization**: Use page breaks when you need to force content onto a new page, especially useful for starting a new chapter or section.

3. **Headers and Footers for Professionalism**: Headers and footers are ideal for adding consistent details like the title, date, or page numbers throughout your document.

Chapter 6. Working with Tables

Creating and Formatting Tables

Creating a Table

Tables help organize information in a structured format, perfect for displaying data clearly.

1. **Insert a Table**:
    o   Go to the **Insert tab** and click **Table** in the **Tables group**.

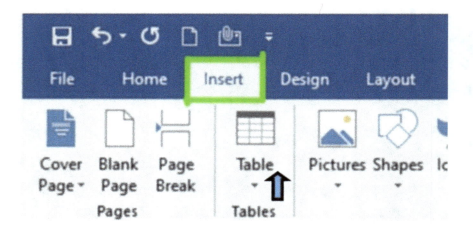

    o   A grid will appear where you can select the number of rows and columns by dragging across the grid.

Alternatively, click **Insert Table** and manually specify the number of rows and columns.

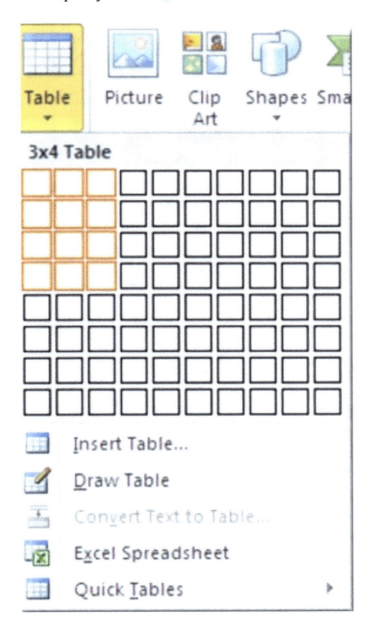

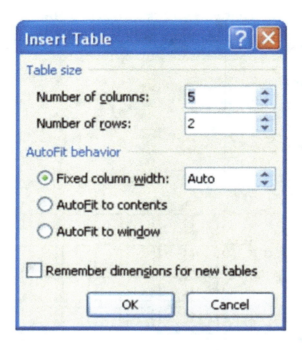

*For more precise control, click **Insert Table***

Formatting a Table

Formatting enhances the appearance of a table, making it easier to read and more visually appealing.

1. **Applying Table Styles**:
   - After inserting the table, click anywhere inside the table to activate the **Table Design** tab.
   - In the **Table Styles** group, choose from predefined table styles such as **Light**, **Medium**, or **Dark**.
   - You can also create your own custom table style by selecting **New Table Style**.

2. **Customizing Table Borders and Shading**:
    - Use the **Borders** dropdown to add or remove borders for individual cells or the entire table.
    - Click **Shading** to apply background color to cells or entire rows.
3. **Adjusting Row and Column Size**:
    - To resize a row or column, hover your cursor over the edge of a row or column until the resize cursor appears (a double-headed arrow), then drag to adjust the size.

Inserting, Deleting, and Merging Cells, Rows, and Columns

Inserting Cells, Rows, and Columns

1. **Insert Cells**:
    - Select the cell where you want new cells to appear.
    - Right-click and choose **Insert**. You can choose to insert cells, shift existing cells left or right, or shift rows/columns up or down.
2. **Insert Rows and Columns**:
    - Right-click on a row number or column letter to insert a row or column before or after the selected one.
    - Alternatively, go to the **Table Tools Layout tab** and click **Insert Above**, **Insert Below**, **Insert Left**, or **Insert Right** in the **Rows & Columns** group.

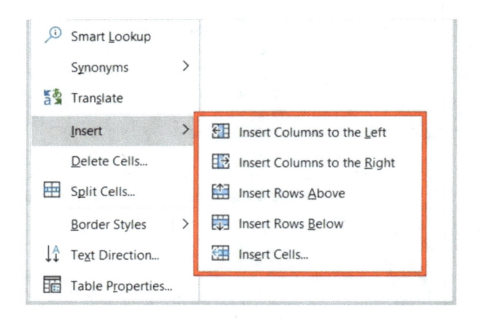

Deleting Cells, Rows, and Columns

1. **Delete Cells**:
   - Select the cell(s) to delete.
   - Right-click and select **Delete Cells**, then choose how you want to shift the remaining cells (e.g., up or left).
2. **Delete Rows and Columns**:
   - Right-click on a row or column, then choose **Delete**.
   - In the submenu, select either **Delete Rows** or **Delete Columns** depending on your choice.

Merging Cells

1. **Merge Cells**:
   - Highlight the cells you want to merge (cells should be adjacent).

- Right-click and select **Merge Cells**. Alternatively, on the **Table Tools Layout tab**, click **Merge Cells** in the **Merge** group.
- Merging cells is often useful for creating headers or grouping related content.

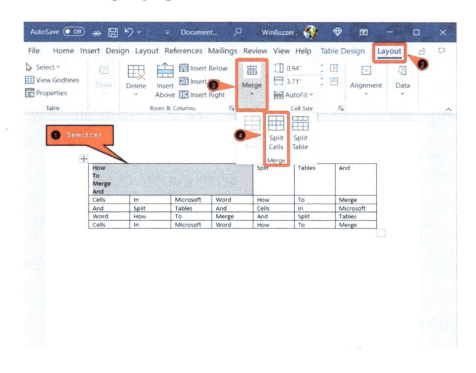

Adjusting Table Alignment and Text Wrapping

Adjusting Table Alignment

Table alignment controls how the table appears on the page and its relationship to surrounding text.

1. **Aligning the Table**:
   - o Select the entire table by clicking the **Table Move Handle** (the four-arrow icon in the top-left corner of the table).
   - o Go to the **Layout tab** under **Table Tools** and click the **Align** button in the **Alignment group**. You can choose from several alignment options:
     - ▪ **Align Left**
     - ▪ **Center**
     - ▪ **Align Right**
     - ▪ **Align Top**, **Center**, or **Bottom** for vertical alignment.
2. **Adjusting Table Position**:
   - o Use the **Table Properties** dialog box to adjust the table's position on the page.
   - o Right-click the table and select **Table Properties**. Under the **Table** tab, choose **Alignment** and select how you want the table to be positioned (Left, Center, Right) relative to the page.

Text Wrapping Around the Table

Text wrapping allows text to flow around the table, creating a more professional look.

1. **Enable Text Wrapping**:
   - o Right-click on the table and select **Table Properties**.
   - o In the **Table Properties** dialog box, go to the **Table** tab.
   - o Under **Text Wrapping**, select **Around**.
2. **Adjust Text Wrapping Settings**:

- Click **Positioning** to fine-tune how text wraps around the table. You can adjust the distance between the table and text from all sides (top, bottom, left, right).
3. **Inserting a Table with Wrap Text Automatically**:
   - If you want text to automatically wrap around your table when it's inserted, use **Insert Table** under the **Insert tab** and enable text wrapping in the **Table Properties** dialog box as described above.

Pro Tips for Beginners

1. **Use Table Styles for Consistency**: Applying a pre-designed table style ensures that your tables are visually consistent and aligned with professional document standards.
2. **Merge Cells for Clean Headers**: Merging cells in the top row can help create clean and concise headers for your tables.
3. **Use Text Wrapping for Flexibility**: Wrapping text around tables allows you to create documents with dynamic layouts, making it easier to fit content without disrupting the flow of the page.

Chapter 7. Inserting Objects and Media

Adding Pictures, Shapes, Icons, and SmartArt

Adding Pictures

Pictures can make your documents more engaging and visually appealing.

1. **Insert a Picture**:
    - o Go to the **Insert tab** and click **Pictures** in the **Illustrations group**.
    - o You can choose to insert a picture from:
        - ▪ **This Device**: Select a picture stored on your computer.
        - ▪ **Stock Images**: Browse stock images offered by Microsoft.
        - ▪ **Online Pictures**: Search for images from the web via the search tool.

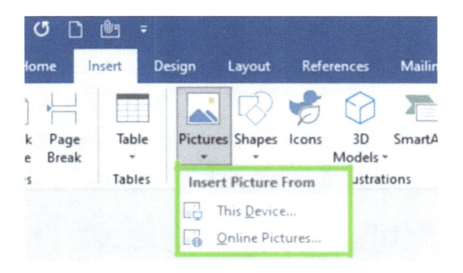

2. **Resizing and Positioning a Picture**:
   - ○ Once the picture is inserted, select it. Resize the image by clicking and dragging the corners.

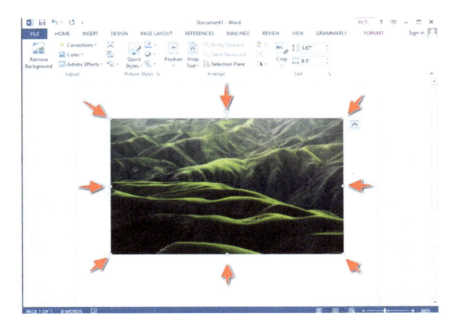

- Use the **Picture Tools Format tab** to change the position, apply text wrapping, or resize the picture.
- To adjust the position, click **Position** in the **Arrange group**, and select your preferred layout.

Adding Shapes

Shapes are used to enhance visual appeal, create diagrams, or provide emphasis in a document.

1. **Insert a Shape**:
   - Go to the **Insert tab** and click **Shapes**.
   - A dropdown list will appear with different types of shapes like rectangles, arrows, lines, stars, and callouts.

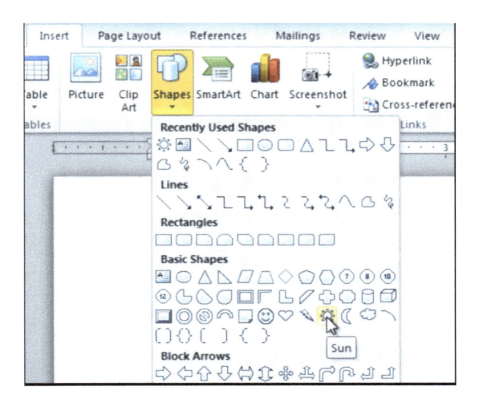

2. **Customizing a Shape**:
   o After inserting the shape, use the **Shape Format tab** to change the fill color, outline, or apply effects like shadow, 3D, and reflection.

Inserting Icons

Icons are small images that represent actions or concepts.

1. **Insert an Icon**:
   o Go to the **Insert tab** and click **Icons** in the **Illustrations group**.

- A collection of icons will open. Use the search bar to find an icon, then click **Insert** to add it to the document.

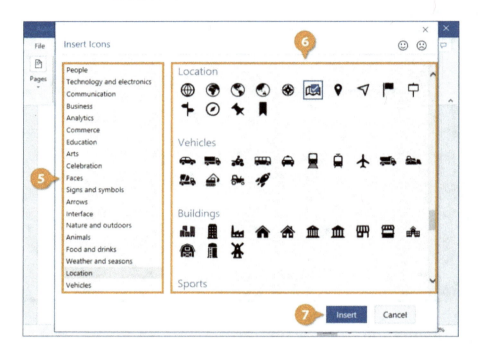

2. **Customizing Icons**:
   - You can resize, rotate, and color the icon using the options in the **Graphics Tools Format tab**.

Inserting SmartArt

SmartArt is a tool to create diagrams that convey information visually, like process flows, hierarchies, or relationships.

1. **Insert SmartArt**:

- Go to the **Insert tab** and click **SmartArt** in the **Illustrations group**.

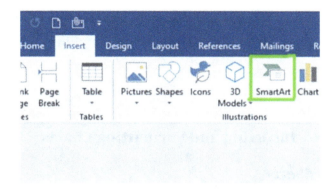

- Choose a SmartArt graphic from the available categories such as **List**, **Process**, **Cycle**, **Hierarchy**, etc.

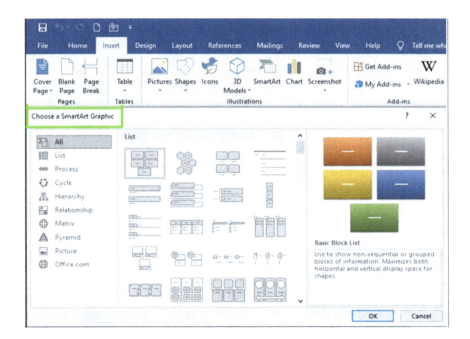

o   Once inserted, you can add text by clicking on the text pane, or directly in the shape areas.

2. **Formatting SmartArt**:
    o   Use the **SmartArt Tools Design** and **Format** tabs to customize the colors, layout, and effects of your SmartArt graphic.

Inserting and Formatting Charts

Inserting a Chart

Charts are helpful for visually representing data and trends.

1. **Insert a Chart**:
    o   Go to the **Insert tab** and click **Chart** in the **Illustrations group**.
    o   A dialog box will open with various chart types, including Column, Line, Pie, and more. Select your desired chart type and click **OK**.
    o   Excel will open in the background with a data table where you can enter your chart data.

Editing and Formatting the Chart

Once your chart is inserted, you can customize it to better display the data.

1. **Edit Chart Data**:
    o   To change the data, click on the chart and select **Edit Data** from the **Chart Tools Design tab**. This will

open the Excel sheet where you can modify the values.

2. **Formatting the Chart**:
   o Use the **Chart Tools Design** and **Format** tabs to:
     ▪ Change the chart style and color scheme.
     ▪ Add chart elements such as titles, legends, data labels, and axes.
     ▪ Adjust the layout to improve clarity and presentation.

Chart Types

1. **Column and Bar Charts**: Ideal for comparing values across categories.
2. **Line Charts**: Best used to show trends over time.
3. **Pie Charts**: Great for showing parts of a whole.
4. **Area and Scatter Charts**: Useful for statistical data and relationships between variables.

Embedding and Linking Excel Data

Embedding Excel Data into Word

Embedding allows you to insert an Excel worksheet into a Word document, preserving the ability to edit data within Word itself.

1. **Embed Excel Data**:
   o Go to the **Insert tab** and click **Object** in the **Text group**.
   o In the **Object dialog box**, select **Create from File**.

- Browse to the Excel file you want to embed and select it.
- Check the **Display as Icon** box if you prefer the object to be shown as an icon rather than an embedded worksheet.

Linking Excel Data to Word

Linking allows you to insert Excel data into Word while maintaining a connection to the original Excel file. Any updates made to the Excel file will be reflected in the Word document.

1. **Link Excel Data**:
   - Copy the data from Excel (select the cells, right-click, and choose **Copy**).
   - In Word, right-click where you want to place the data and select **Paste Special**.
   - In the dialog box, select **Paste Link** and choose **Microsoft Excel Worksheet Object**.
   - The data will appear in Word, and any updates made in Excel will automatically reflect in the Word document.

Updating Linked Excel Data

1. **Refresh Linked Data**:
   - If the data in the linked Excel file has been changed, right-click on the linked data in Word and choose **Update Link** to ensure it reflects the latest changes.

Pro Tips for Beginners

1. **Use Icons and SmartArt to Break Up Text**: When writing long documents, inserting icons or SmartArt can help break up dense sections of text, making the document more engaging and easier to navigate.
2. **Embed Data for Easy Access**: When working with both Word and Excel, embedding Excel data into Word is a great way to keep all your information in one place without needing to open multiple files.
3. **Be Mindful of Chart Types**: Different chart types suit different kinds of data, so choose the one that best represents the message you're trying to convey. For instance, pie charts work well for parts-of-a-whole data, while line charts excel at showing trends over time.

Chapter 8. Proofing and Reviewing Documents

Using Spell Check, Grammar Check, and Thesaurus

Using Spell Check

Spell check helps identify and correct spelling errors in your document.

1. **Run Spell Check Automatically**:
   - As you type, Word will automatically underline misspelled words with a **red squiggly line**.
   - Right-click on the underlined word to see suggestions and click on the correct word to replace it.
2. **Run Spell Check Manually**:
   - Go to the **Review tab** and click **Spelling & Grammar** in the **Proofing group**.
   - Word will begin checking the entire document, highlighting errors, and offering corrections. You can choose to **Ignore**, **Ignore All**, or **Change** each error.

Using Grammar Check

Grammar check identifies grammatical mistakes, such as sentence structure issues or subject-verb agreement problems.

1. **Grammar Check Settings**:
   - In the **Spelling & Grammar** dialog box, you can adjust settings by clicking **Options**. Here, you can choose to have Word check for grammar issues, such as fragmented sentences or misplaced commas.
2. **Fixing Grammar Issues**:
   - Word will highlight grammar errors with a **blue squiggly line**. Right-click to view suggested corrections and choose the one that applies.

Using the Thesaurus

The Thesaurus tool helps you find synonyms to avoid repetition or to enhance your vocabulary.

1. **Using the Thesaurus**:
   - Select the word you want to find a synonym for, then right-click and choose **Synonyms** from the context menu.
   - A list of suggested synonyms will appear. You can select the one that fits your needs.
2. **Thesaurus in the Review Tab**:
   - Go to the **Review tab** and click **Thesaurus** in the **Proofing group**. This opens a pane where you can search for synonyms and antonyms for any word.

Adding Comments and Using Track Changes

Adding Comments

Comments are useful for leaving notes or suggestions in a document, without altering the text itself.

1. **Insert a Comment**:
   - Highlight the text you want to comment on, then go to the **Review tab** and click **New Comment** in the **Comments group**.

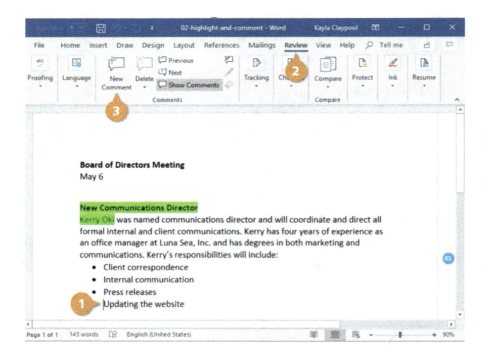

   - A comment balloon will appear in the margin, where you can type your comment.

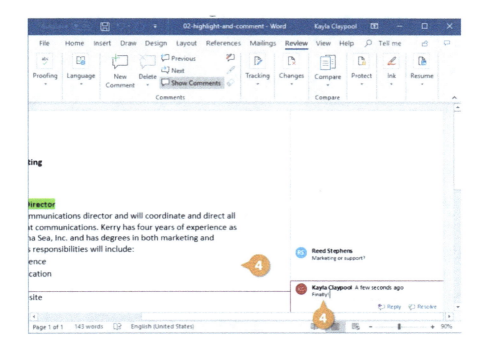

2. **Replying to Comments**:

    ○ To reply to a comment, click the **Reply** button in the comment balloon, then type your response.

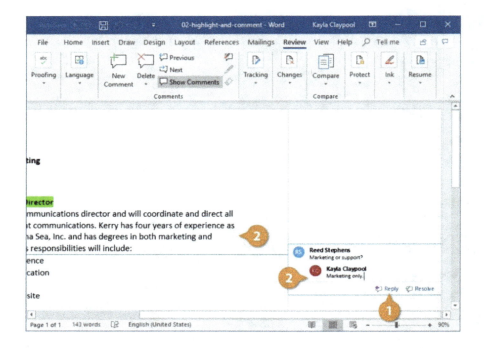

3. **Navigating Through Comments**:
   o Use the **Previous** and **Next** buttons in the **Comments group** to cycle through all comments in the document.

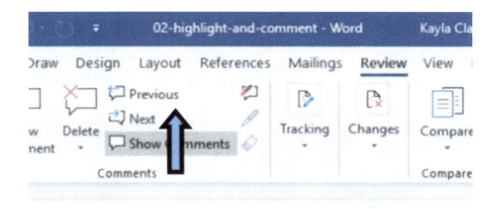

Using Track Changes

Track Changes allows you to track edits and revisions made to the document, which is especially useful for collaboration.

1. **Enable Track Changes**:
   - Go to the **Review tab** and click **Track Changes** in the **Tracking group**. Once enabled, all changes (insertions, deletions, formatting changes) will be highlighted.

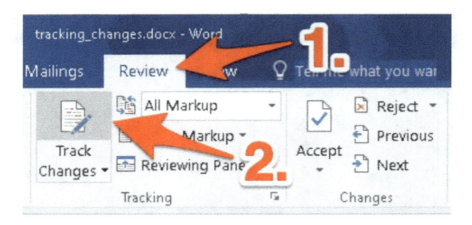

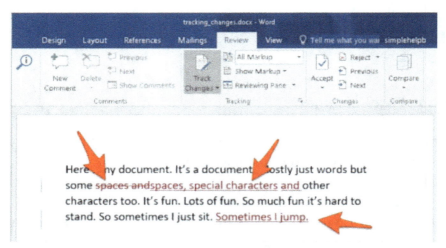

2. **Viewing Changes**:
   o Edits made by different people are usually color-coded. Inserted text appears underlined, while deleted text appears struck through.
   o You can choose how changes are displayed by clicking on the **Tracking** dropdown and selecting the desired view (e.g., **Simple Markup**, **All Markup**, or **No Markup**).

3. **Accepting or Rejecting Changes**:
   - To finalize edits, go to the **Review tab** and use the **Accept** or **Reject** buttons in the **Changes group**.
   - You can accept or reject changes one by one, or choose **Accept All Changes** to approve everything at once.

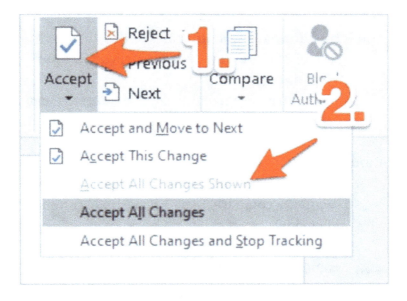

4. **Show/Hide Track Changes**:
   - If you want to hide tracked changes temporarily, select **No Markup** in the **Tracking group**. To show all changes again, select **All Markup**.

Comparing and Combining Documents

Comparing Documents

Word allows you to compare two versions of a document to highlight differences. This is particularly useful when working on revisions or collaborating with others.

1. **Open the Compare Documents Tool**:
    o Go to the **Review tab** and click **Compare** in the **Compare group**.
    o In the dropdown menu, choose **Compare** again. This opens a dialog box where you can select the two documents you wish to compare.
2. **Compare Settings**:
    o In the dialog box, choose what kind of changes you want to compare (e.g., formatting, comments, text changes).
    o After selecting the documents, click **OK**. Word will generate a new document showing both the original and revised versions, with changes highlighted.

Combining Documents

If you have multiple versions of a document and want to merge them, the **Combine Documents** feature can help.

1. **Combine Documents**:
    o In the **Review tab**, click **Compare**, then choose **Combine** from the dropdown menu.
    o In the **Combine Documents** dialog box, select the original and revised documents.

o Word will merge the changes, highlighting differences between the documents in a new combined version.

2. **Accepting or Rejecting Combined Changes**:
    o Just like with Track Changes, you can accept or reject individual changes or all changes at once.

Pro Tips for Beginners

1. **Use Track Changes for Collaboration**: Track Changes is an excellent tool for reviewing documents with others. It helps maintain transparency and ensures everyone's input is visible.

2. **Proofing Tools for Efficiency**: Use the **Spelling & Grammar** tool alongside the **Thesaurus** to polish your writing. It can also save time by automatically finding and correcting common errors.

3. **Accept or Reject Changes Carefully**: When working with tracked changes, make sure you carefully review each change before accepting it. This ensures the final version is clean and accurate.

4. **Combining Documents**: When merging multiple versions of a document, always double-check the combined file for any errors that might have been introduced in the process.

Chapter 9. Using Advanced Features

Introduction to Mail Merge

What is Mail Merge?

Mail Merge is a powerful feature in Microsoft Word that allows you to create multiple documents based on a template, automatically inserting personalized data from an external source, like a database or spreadsheet. This feature is often used for creating form letters, envelopes, labels, and other documents that require repetitive information.

Creating Letters with Mail Merge

1. **Prepare Your Data Source**:
   - The first step in using Mail Merge is to have a data source, typically an **Excel spreadsheet** or **Access database**. This data source should include the names, addresses, or other information you want to insert into your letters.
   - Ensure the data is organized into columns (e.g., First Name, Last Name, Address, City, etc.) with appropriate headings.
2. **Start the Mail Merge**:
   - Go to the **Mailings tab** in Word and click **Start Mail Merge**. Select **Letters** from the dropdown options.

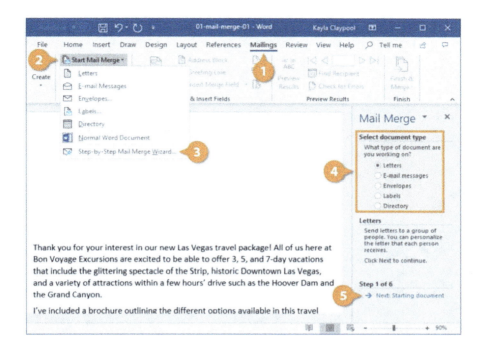

o Choose **Select Recipients** and then click **Use an Existing List** to browse and select your data source (Excel file or Access database).

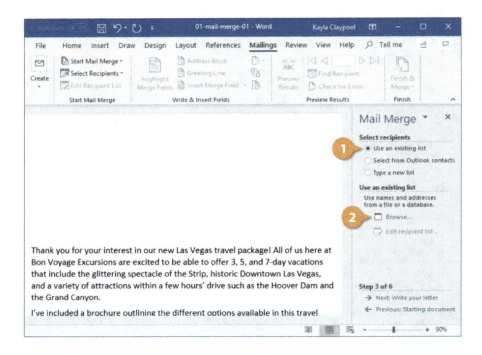

3. **Insert Merge Fields**:
   - ○ Place your cursor where you want personalized data (such as a name or address) to appear in the letter.
   - ○ Click **Insert Merge Field** in the **Mailings tab**, and choose the appropriate field from your data source (e.g., First Name, Last Name, etc.).
   - ○ The merge field will appear in your document like this: «First Name».
4. **Preview Your Document**:
   - ○ Click **Preview Results** to see how the merged data will appear in your document. Word will display the first record from your data source, and you can navigate through other records using the arrow buttons.
5. **Complete the Mail Merge**:

- Once you're satisfied with the letter, click **Finish & Merge** in the **Mailings tab**. You can choose to either print the letters directly or generate a new document containing all the merged letters.

Creating Envelopes and Labels

1. **Start Mail Merge for Envelopes**:
   - Follow the same steps as for letters, but choose **Envelopes** instead of **Letters** from the **Start Mail Merge** dropdown.
   - Select the envelope size (e.g., #10) by clicking **Envelopes** and choosing the appropriate size in the dialog box.
2. **Insert Address Fields**:
   - Once your data source is connected, click **Insert Merge Field** and choose the fields that will be used in the envelope (such as Address, City, and Zip Code).
3. **Preview and Print**:
   - Preview the envelopes to ensure they look correct.
   - When ready, select **Finish & Merge** to either print the envelopes directly or create a new document with all the merged addresses.
4. **Creating Labels**:
   - Similar to creating envelopes, but choose **Labels** from the **Start Mail Merge** dropdown.

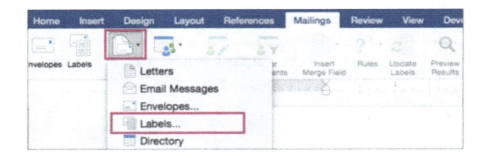

- o Select your preferred label size (e.g., Avery 5160), and proceed with inserting the necessary address fields.

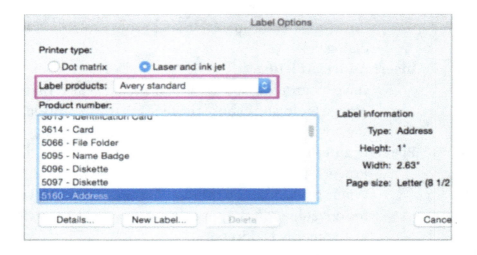

Creating and Using Bookmarks and Cross-References

What Are Bookmarks?

Bookmarks are useful for creating hyperlinks to specific sections of a document or for referencing content without having to scroll through the entire document. They can be used to navigate large documents or link to frequently used areas.

1. **Creating a Bookmark**:
   o Place your cursor where you want to create a bookmark.
   o Go to the **Insert tab** and click **Bookmark** in the **Links group**.
   o In the **Bookmark dialog box**, give your bookmark a name (no spaces allowed), then click **Add**.
2. **Using Bookmarks**:
   o To link to a bookmark, highlight the text or image where you want to insert the link.
   o Go to the **Insert tab**, click **Link**, and select **Place in This Document**.
   o A list of your bookmarks will appear. Select the appropriate bookmark, and Word will create a hyperlink to that section.

What Are Cross-References?

Cross-references allow you to refer to other sections of your document, such as headings, figure numbers, or tables. When the target of a cross-reference changes (e.g., a heading moves or a figure number changes), the cross-reference updates automatically.

1. **Inserting a Cross-Reference**:
   o Place your cursor where you want to insert the cross-reference.
   o Go to the **Insert tab**, click **Cross-reference** in the **Links group**.

- o In the **Cross-reference dialog box**, select the type of reference (e.g., Heading, Figure, Table).
- o Select the specific item you want to reference and click **Insert**. The reference will appear as a hyperlink that updates if the referenced item changes.

2. **Using Cross-References for Navigation**:
   - o Cross-references are particularly useful in large documents, such as reports or academic papers, to provide easy navigation to key sections.

Generating a Table of Contents and Index

Creating a Table of Contents (TOC)

A Table of Contents is automatically generated based on your document's headings and subheadings. It serves as a roadmap for readers, helping them navigate longer documents.

1. **Apply Heading Styles**:
   - o Before creating a TOC, apply the built-in heading styles to the sections and subsections of your document. Go to the **Home tab** and select a heading style (e.g., **Heading 1**, **Heading 2**, **Heading 3**) for each section.

2. **Insert the TOC**:
   - o Place your cursor where you want the TOC to appear (typically at the beginning of the document).
   - o Go to the **References tab** and click **Table of Contents**.

- Choose a style for the TOC from the dropdown (e.g., **Automatic Table 1** or **Manual Table**).
3. **Updating the TOC**:
   - If you add or remove content in the document, the TOC won't automatically update. To refresh it, right-click on the TOC and select **Update Field**. You can choose to update only the page numbers or the entire TOC.

Creating an Index

An Index is a list of keywords or topics found in your document, along with the page numbers where they appear. It's typically placed at the end of the document.

1. **Mark Index Entries**:
   - Highlight the word or phrase you want to include in the index.
   - Go to the **References tab** and click **Mark Entry** in the **Index group**. This opens the **Mark Index Entry dialog box**.
   - Choose whether to mark the word itself or a range of text, and click **Mark**. Repeat for other entries.
2. **Insert the Index**:
   - Once you've marked all the necessary entries, place your cursor where you want the index to appear (usually at the end of the document).
   - Go to the **References tab**, click **Insert Index** in the **Index group**.

- o   Select the format and style for the index, and click **OK**. Word will automatically generate an index based on the entries you've marked.

3. **Updating the Index**:
   - o   If you make changes to the document after inserting the index (e.g., adding or removing entries), you can update it by right-clicking on the index and selecting **Update Field**.

Pro Tips for Beginners

1. **Mail Merge for Personalization**: Use Mail Merge to easily create personalized letters, invitations, or labels for events or marketing purposes. Make sure your data source is well-organized to ensure smooth merges.

2. **Efficient Cross-References**: Use cross-references in lengthy documents to avoid manually updating references, especially when section titles or figure numbers change.

3. **Table of Contents for Large Documents**: Always use heading styles and let Word generate your TOC to save time and keep everything organized. Don't forget to update it regularly.

4. **Indexing Your Document**: If you're writing a research paper or a book, indexing can be a helpful way to allow readers to quickly locate important topics.

Chapter 10. Exporting and Printing Documents

Saving Documents in Different Formats

Microsoft Word allows you to save your documents in various formats to suit different needs. Whether you need a standard Word file for editing or a PDF for sharing, Word makes it easy to export your document in the format you require.

Steps to Save in Different Formats:

1. **Save as a Word Document (.docx)**:
   - By default, Word saves your document in the **.docx** format. This is the standard format for Word documents, and it retains all the features of Word (e.g., formatting, images, tables).
   - To save in this format, simply go to the **File tab** > **Save As** > select the location (e.g., **This PC**, **OneDrive**) and click **Save**.
2. **Save as a PDF (.pdf)**:
   - PDFs are a widely used format for sharing documents as they preserve formatting and are not easily editable.
   - To save as a PDF, go to **File tab** > **Save As** > select the desired location, then from the **Save as type** dropdown menu, choose **PDF**.

- o Click **Save**. This is particularly useful for documents you intend to share or publish.
3. **Save as an Older Version of Word**:
   - o If you need to save your document in an older format (e.g., **.doc**), go to the **File tab** > **Save As** > choose **Word 97-2003 Document** from the **Save as type** dropdown. This ensures that users with older versions of Word can open and read your document.
4. **Save as a Text File (.txt)**:
   - o If you only need the plain text from your document and don't require any formatting, you can save it as a **.txt** file. To do this, go to **File tab** > **Save As** > **Plain Text**.
   - o This will strip all the formatting and leave you with a clean text file.
5. **Save as an HTML File**:
   - o If you plan to upload your document to a website or convert it into a webpage, you can save it as an **HTML** file.
   - o Go to **File tab** > **Save As** > choose **Web Page** or **Single File Web Page**. This converts your document into an HTML format suitable for web publishing.
6. **Save as an Image**:
   - o Word also allows you to save documents as images, such as PNG or JPEG, by first converting the document to a PDF and then using a screenshot or online converter to save each page as an image.

Setting Up Print Options (Page Range, Duplex Printing, Scaling)

Before printing, it's important to configure your print options to ensure that the document prints exactly as you expect, whether it's choosing specific pages, duplex printing (double-sided), or adjusting the document's scaling.

Steps to Set Up Print Options:

1. **Select Your Printer**:
   - Go to the **File tab** and click on **Print**. This opens the print setup menu where you can select the printer.

   - If you have multiple printers, use the **Printer dropdown** to choose the printer you want to use.
2. **Page Range**:
   - To print specific pages of the document, under the **Pages** section, you can select:
     - **All Pages** to print the entire document.
     - **Pages** to print a custom range (e.g., 1-3, 7-10).
     - **Current Page** to print only the page currently visible on the screen.
   - To enter a range, type the starting and ending page numbers separated by a dash (e.g., 1-5).

3. **Duplex Printing (Double-Sided)**:
   - If your printer supports duplex (double-sided) printing, you can select this option in the print settings.
   - Look for a dropdown or checkbox called **Print on Both Sides** or **Duplex Printing**. Choose **Long-edge binding** or **Short-edge binding**, depending on how you want the pages oriented.
   - If you don't see this option, it could mean your printer doesn't support duplex printing.
4. **Scaling Options**:
   - **Fit to One Page**: If you want the document to fit onto a single page, you can choose **Scale to Paper Size** and select **Fit to One Page**.
   - **Multiple Pages Per Sheet**: If you want to print multiple pages on a single sheet of paper (e.g., 2 pages per sheet), you can select **Multiple Pages per Sheet** from the print options. This is useful for saving paper or creating handouts.
   - **Custom Scaling**: If your document contains large images or charts and you want to reduce the content size to fit the page, choose **Custom Scaling** options and adjust the scaling percentage.
5. **Color Options**:
   - Under the **Color** dropdown, you can select whether to print in **Color**, **Black and White**, or **Grayscale**, depending on your printer's capabilities and your needs.
6. **Other Options**:
   - If needed, you can also adjust the **Paper Size** and **Orientation** (Portrait or Landscape) before printing.

o Some printers offer additional settings like **Watermark** or **Quality** adjustments, which you can configure from the **Print Setup** dialog.

Printing a Document

Once you have set up all your print options, it's time to print your document.

Steps to Print:

1. **Preview the Document**:

- o Before printing, you can click **Preview** in the print menu to see how your document will appear on paper. This is especially useful to check for any formatting issues or errors before wasting paper and ink.

2. **Select the Number of Copies**:
   - o In the **Copies** box, enter the number of copies you want to print. Most printers will allow you to print multiple copies at once.

3. **Choose Printer Settings**:
   - o Select the correct **printer** from the printer dropdown. If you're printing to a PDF or virtual printer, make sure to choose the right one.

4. **Print the Document**:
   - o Once everything looks good, click the **Print** button to start the printing process.
   - o Your document will be sent to the printer, and you should receive your printed pages shortly.

5. **Cancel or Pause Printing**:
   - o If you need to stop the printing process for any reason, go to the **Print queue** on your computer (usually accessible from the **Devices and Printers** menu) and cancel or pause the print job.

Pro Tips for Beginners:

1. **Saving as PDF for Sharing**: If you need to send a document but don't want others to easily make changes, saving it as a PDF is a great option.

2. **Use Print Preview**: Always use **Print Preview** to ensure your document looks correct before wasting paper and ink. This will help catch issues with page breaks, alignment, and scaling.
3. **Set Up Duplex Printing**: If your printer supports duplex printing, it's an eco-friendly and cost-effective way to print double-sided documents. Ensure your document is formatted accordingly (e.g., no odd-numbered pages that don't match up with even-numbered pages).
4. **Reduce Paper Waste with Multiple Pages per Sheet**: When printing drafts or notes, consider printing multiple pages per sheet. This saves paper and is especially handy for reviewing lengthy documents.
5. **Stay Organized with Page Ranges**: If you're printing a large document, you can print specific sections (e.g., chapters or headings) to keep track of changes or updates without printing everything.

Part 2: Microsoft Excel for Beginners

Chapter 1. Introduction to Microsoft Excel

What is Microsoft Excel?

Microsoft Excel is a powerful spreadsheet software program used for organizing, analyzing, and visualizing data. It is part of the Microsoft Office Suite and is widely used across different industries for tasks such as financial analysis, data management, budgeting, and project planning.

Excel allows you to store data in cells that are organized into rows and columns. These cells can contain various types of data, including numbers, text, dates, and formulas. With Excel, you can perform complex calculations, create charts and graphs, and automate tasks through macros and advanced functions.

Excel's Core Functions:

- **Data Entry**: Easily enter and organize data in a tabular format.
- **Formulas and Functions**: Perform calculations automatically using built-in functions like SUM, AVERAGE, IF, etc.
- **Charts and Graphs**: Visualize data in various chart formats, including bar charts, pie charts, and line graphs.

- **Data Analysis**: Use tools like PivotTables and Power Query to summarize and analyze large datasets.
- **Automation**: Use Excel's macro capabilities (VBA) to automate repetitive tasks and calculations.

Overview of Key Features and Use Cases

Microsoft Excel is used by individuals and organizations alike for a wide variety of tasks. Some of its key features and use cases include:

1. **Data Organization**:
   - Excel allows you to organize large sets of data in tables, making it easier to read, analyze, and manage.
   - Each document in Excel is referred to as a **workbook**, which contains **worksheets**—individual sheets where you input and manage data.
2. **Mathematical Calculations**:
   - Excel provides a comprehensive set of built-in mathematical functions, ranging from basic operations like addition and subtraction to complex calculations such as statistical analysis and financial modeling.
3. **Data Analysis**:
   - With features like **PivotTables**, **Power Query**, and **Data Validation**, Excel helps users analyze data, look for trends, and make data-driven decisions.
   - It also offers tools like **Conditional Formatting**, which allows you to visually highlight key data points based on specific conditions.

4. **Charting and Visualization**:
   - Excel allows you to convert your data into meaningful charts and graphs. With a wide selection of chart types (e.g., bar, line, pie, scatter), it's easy to create professional-looking visuals that help you and your audience understand the data quickly.
5. **Collaboration**:
   - With cloud integration, Excel allows for collaborative work, enabling multiple people to work on the same document simultaneously in real-time (via OneDrive or SharePoint).
   - It also supports commenting and version control, so users can track changes and communicate within the workbook.
6. **Task Automation**:
   - Excel's **macros** (programmed using Visual Basic for Applications – VBA) allow users to automate repetitive tasks, improving efficiency in workflows.
7. **Financial Modeling and Budgeting**:
   - Excel is widely used for creating **financial models**, tracking **budgets**, and performing **forecasting** and **accounting** calculations.
   - It also supports **what-if analysis** with tools like **Scenario Manager** and **Goal Seek**.

System Requirements and Installation

To use Microsoft Excel, your system must meet the minimum requirements specified by Microsoft. Here's an overview:

Windows:

- **Operating System**: Windows 10, Windows 11 (or later)
- **Processor**: 1.6 GHz or faster processor (32-bit or 64-bit)
- **RAM**: 4 GB (32-bit) or 8 GB (64-bit)

- **Hard Disk**: At least 4 GB of available disk space
- **Display**: 1280 x 800 screen resolution
- **Graphics**: DirectX 9 or later with WDDM 2.0 driver
- **Internet**: Internet connection for updates, product activation, and cloud features

Mac:

- **Operating System**: macOS 2019 or later
- **Processor**: Intel or Apple M1/M2 chip
- **RAM**: 4 GB or more
- **Hard Disk**: At least 10 GB of available disk space
- **Display**: 1280 x 800 screen resolution
- **Graphics**: Graphics card with Metal support
- **Internet**: Internet connection for updates, product activation, and cloud features

Installation Process:

1. **Download**:
   - You can download Microsoft Excel as part of the **Microsoft Office suite** or subscribe to **Microsoft 365**.
   - Go to the official Microsoft website to download Excel or purchase Microsoft 365.
2. **Install**:
   - After downloading, open the installation file. Follow the on-screen instructions to install Microsoft Excel.
   - Depending on your version (Office 365, Office 2021, etc.), the steps may vary slightly.
3. **Activate**:

- After installation, you may need to activate Excel by signing in with your **Microsoft account** or entering a product key.
- If you are using Microsoft 365, sign in with your Microsoft account to enable cloud features.

Understanding the Excel Interface

The Excel interface is designed to make it easy for users to navigate and access various tools and features. Let's break it down into its major components:

Workbook, Worksheet, and Gridlines

- **Workbook**: An Excel file is called a **workbook**. It contains one or more **worksheets**, which are individual pages where you work with data.
  - Each workbook can hold an unlimited number of worksheets, which you can switch between using the tabs at the bottom.
- **Worksheet**: A **worksheet** consists of a grid of cells arranged into rows and columns.
  - Rows are numbered (1, 2, 3...), while columns are labeled with letters (A, B, C...).
  - Each cell is identified by its unique address (e.g., A1, B3), which is a combination of its column letter and row number.
- **Gridlines**:

- The **gridlines** are the light grey lines that separate the cells in a worksheet. They help guide the placement of data and make it easier to navigate the spreadsheet.
- Gridlines don't appear when you print the document unless specifically enabled.

Ribbon, Quick Access Toolbar, and Status Bar

1. **Ribbon**:
   - The **Ribbon** is the large set of tabs at the top of the Excel window that contains most of the tools and features in Excel. It is divided into several tabs like **Home**, **Insert**, **Formulas**, and **Data**, each containing relevant groups of commands.
   - Each tab on the Ribbon houses a set of tools related to specific tasks. For example:
     - **Home tab**: Contains basic tools like formatting, alignment, and clipboard commands (Copy, Paste).
     - **Insert tab**: Lets you add charts, tables, pictures, and more.
     - **Formulas tab**: Provides a wide array of mathematical and financial functions.

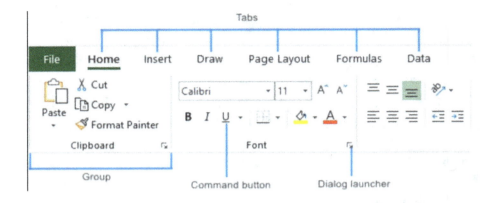

2. **Quick Access Toolbar**:
   o The **Quick Access Toolbar** is located at the top left corner of the Excel window, above the Ribbon. It provides fast access to frequently used commands like **Save**, **Undo**, and **Redo**.
   o You can customize this toolbar by adding or removing commands. Simply click the small dropdown arrow next to the toolbar and choose **More Commands** to modify it.

102

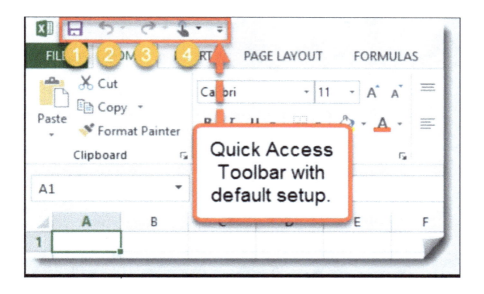

Quick Access Toolbar with default setup.

3. **Status Bar**:
   o The **Status Bar** is located at the bottom of the Excel window, and it provides important information about your current worksheet.
   o The Status Bar displays things like the **average**, **sum**, and **count** of selected data, as well as information about your document's zoom level, page layout, and the current mode (e.g., ready, edit).

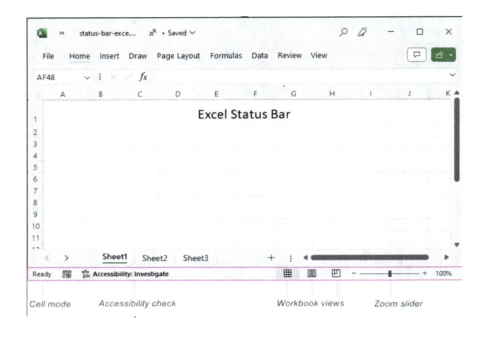

Pro Tips for Beginners:

1. **Mastering the Ribbon**: Familiarize yourself with the Ribbon, as it contains most of the features you'll use frequently. Hovering over any command shows a tooltip with a brief description of what it does.

2. **Use Quick Access Toolbar**: Add your most-used commands to the Quick Access Toolbar for faster access. You can add things like **New**, **Save**, and **Print** for more convenience.

3. **Explore the Status Bar**: Keep an eye on the Status Bar to track the progress of your current tasks, like the sum of selected numbers or the zoom level. You can also customize what information appears in the Status Bar by right-clicking

on it and selecting options like **Average** or **Numerical Count**.

Chapter 2. Getting Started with Excel

Creating a New Workbook

Creating a new workbook in Microsoft Excel is quick and easy, and it's the first step to begin entering and organizing your data. Here's how to create a new workbook:

1. **Using the Start Screen**:
   - When you open Excel, you'll be presented with the **Start Screen**. Here, you can choose a template or create a **Blank Workbook**.
     - To create a blank workbook, click the **Blank Workbook** option in the Start Screen.
     - If you wish to use a template, click on a template from the available options (e.g., budgets, invoices, calendars).
2. **From the Ribbon**:
   - You can also create a new workbook from any existing workbook:
     - Go to the **File** tab on the Ribbon, select **New**, then choose **Blank Workbook** or a template.

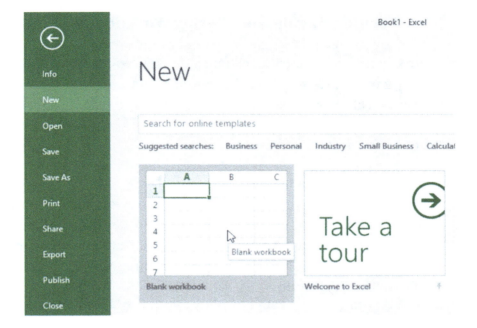

3. **Keyboard Shortcut**:
   - A quicker method to create a new workbook is by pressing **Ctrl + N**.
4. **Using Excel Online**:
   - If you have a Microsoft account, you can create a workbook online through **OneDrive** or **SharePoint**. This method also enables real-time collaboration with others.

Once created, the new workbook will automatically open as a new window or tab, ready for you to begin adding data.

Opening, Saving, and Closing Workbooks

Efficiently managing your workbooks is key to keeping your projects organized. Here's a breakdown of how to open, save, and close your workbooks in Excel.

Opening a Workbook:

1. **From the Start Screen**:
   - When you first open Excel, you can select a workbook from the **Recent** list or click **Open Other Workbooks** to find a workbook stored on your computer or cloud (OneDrive, SharePoint).
2. **From the File Menu**:
   - Click on the **File** tab in the Ribbon and select **Open**. This will allow you to browse and locate an existing file on your computer or a network location.
3. **Keyboard Shortcut**:
   - Use **Ctrl + O** to quickly open the file dialog and browse for an existing workbook.

Saving a Workbook:

1. **Saving for the First Time**:
   - When you create a new workbook, it's important to save it immediately to avoid losing data.
   - To save, go to the **File** tab and click **Save As**. Choose the location where you want to store the file (your computer, OneDrive, etc.), give the file a name, and choose a file format (explained in the next section).
2. **Saving Changes**:

- o To save changes to an already-saved workbook, simply click **Save** in the **Quick Access Toolbar** or press **Ctrl + S**.

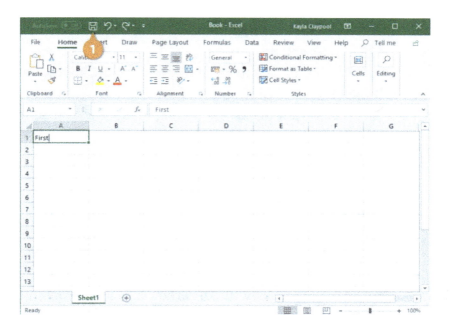

3. **AutoSave (Microsoft 365)**:
   - o If you are using Microsoft 365 and your workbook is stored in OneDrive or SharePoint, you can enable **AutoSave**, which automatically saves your changes as you make them.

Closing a Workbook:

1. **Close Button**:
   - o To close a workbook, click the **X** in the upper-right corner of the workbook window.

- If you have unsaved changes, Excel will prompt you to save them before closing.
2. **Using the File Menu**:
   - Go to the **File** tab and click **Close** to close the workbook without quitting Excel.
3. **Keyboard Shortcut**:
   - Press **Ctrl + W** to close the current workbook.
4. **Exit Excel**:
   - If you want to exit Excel completely, click the **X** in the top-right corner of the Excel window, or use **Alt + F4**.

Understanding File Formats (.xlsx, .xlsm, .csv)

When saving workbooks in Excel, you'll encounter various file formats. Understanding these formats is important to ensure your workbooks are compatible with different Excel versions, other programs, or users.

.xlsx (Excel Workbook):

- This is the default file format for workbooks created in Excel 2007 and later versions.
- **Characteristics**:
  - Supports all Excel features such as formulas, charts, and formatting.
  - Saves data in an XML-based format that is compressed to reduce file size.
  - **Recommended Format** for most users, as it's compatible with modern versions of Excel.

.xlsm (Excel Macro-Enabled Workbook):

- This format is similar to **.xlsx**, but it allows you to store and use **macros**—sets of instructions written in VBA (Visual Basic for Applications) that automate tasks.
- **Characteristics**:
  - If your workbook contains macros (custom VBA code), you must save it in **.xlsm** format to retain the macros.
  - **Important**: Macros in Excel can automate repetitive tasks and improve efficiency but can contain potentially harmful code, so only enable macros from trusted sources.

.csv (Comma Separated Values):

- A **CSV** file is a plain text file that stores data in a tabular format, separated by commas.
- **Characteristics**:
  - Each row of the CSV file represents a row in the Excel worksheet, and each column is separated by a comma.
  - **Limitations**:
    - Doesn't support formatting, formulas, or multiple sheets.
    - Great for exporting data to use in other programs or databases (e.g., Google Sheets, database management systems).
  - **When to use**: When you need to export data for use in other applications or need a lightweight version of your data.

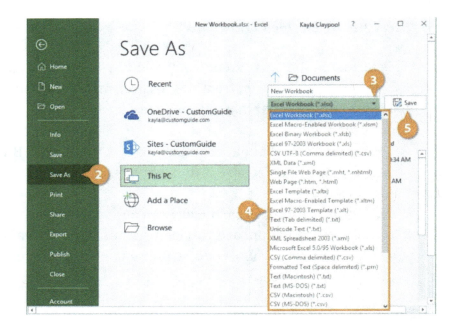

AutoRecover and Version History

Managing file recovery and tracking changes in Excel are crucial, especially when working with large or important workbooks. Excel offers **AutoRecover** and **Version History** to ensure you don't lose your work.

AutoRecover:

- **AutoRecover** is a feature that automatically saves temporary versions of your workbook at regular intervals while you are working. This helps recover your work if Excel crashes or if you forget to save your document.

1. **How It Works**:
    -   By default, Excel saves your work every 10 minutes. You can change this interval in Excel's settings.
    -   If Excel crashes or if your system shuts down unexpectedly, the next time you open Excel, it will offer to recover the last AutoSaved version of your workbook.
2. **How to Use AutoRecover**:
    -   If Excel detects an issue and the workbook wasn't saved, you will be presented with the AutoRecovered version when reopening Excel.
    -   You can also access AutoRecovered files by going to **File → Info → Manage Workbook → Recover Unsaved Workbooks**.

Version History:

-   **Version History** is a feature available with cloud storage services like OneDrive and SharePoint, which tracks changes made to a workbook over time.

1. **How It Works**:
    -   Each time you save your workbook (especially when using OneDrive or SharePoint), Excel saves a new version. You can access previous versions of your workbook, compare them, or restore an older version.
2. **Accessing Version History**:
    -   To view previous versions of a workbook, go to **File → Info → Version History**.

- o You can browse through the versions and click on one to view or restore it.
3. **When to Use**:
    - o Use **Version History** to recover older versions of your workbook if you made unintended changes or want to compare changes over time.
    - o It is a lifesaver when collaborating with others or working on large documents.

Pro Tips for Beginners:

- **Regular Saving**: Make a habit of pressing **Ctrl + S** frequently to avoid losing data.
- **Use AutoSave**: If you're working in the cloud (OneDrive or SharePoint), enable AutoSave to avoid worrying about manually saving your work.
- **Backups**: Use **File → Save As** to create backup copies of your important workbooks, especially before making major changes.
- **Backup Version History**: If you work with critical data, consider storing files on OneDrive or SharePoint to benefit from Version History and AutoRecover features.

Chapter 3. Working with Data in Excel

Entering and Editing Data in Cells

In Excel, cells are the fundamental building blocks where you enter your data. Understanding how to efficiently enter and edit data will greatly improve your productivity. Here's a step-by-step guide for working with data in cells:

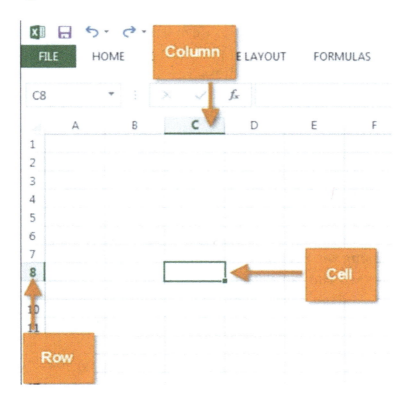

Entering Data:

1. **Click on a Cell**:
   o To start entering data, click on any cell in your worksheet. Cells are identified by a **row** number (e.g., 1, 2, 3) and a **column** letter (e.g., A, B, C). The intersection of these two gives the cell's address (e.g., A1, B3).

2. **Start Typing**:
   o Once the cell is selected, just start typing your data (text, numbers, or dates). Excel will automatically display the text as you type.

3. **Confirm Entry**:
   o Press **Enter** to confirm the entry and move down to the next cell.
   o Alternatively, press **Tab** to move to the next cell to the right, or use the **Arrow Keys** to move to a different cell.

Editing Data:

1. **Click the Cell**:
   o Double-click on the cell you want to edit, or select the cell and start typing to replace the existing data.

2. **Using the Formula Bar**:
   o You can also edit the data in the **Formula Bar** at the top of the window. Click the formula bar, edit the content, and press **Enter** when done.

3. **Delete or Clear Content**:
   o Select the cell and press the **Delete** key to remove the data.

- For more options, right-click on the cell, then choose **Clear Contents** to remove data without affecting the cell formatting.
4. **Undo Changes**:
   - If you make a mistake, you can easily undo changes by pressing **Ctrl + Z** or using the **Undo** button on the Quick Access Toolbar.

Copying, Cutting, Pasting, and Filling Data

Excel provides several ways to manipulate your data, including copying, cutting, pasting, and filling. Here's how to do it:

Copying and Pasting Data:

1. **Copying**:
   - Select the cell or range of cells that you want to copy.
   - Right-click and choose **Copy**, or press **Ctrl + C**.
2. **Pasting**:
   - Select the destination cell where you want the copied data to appear.
   - Right-click and choose **Paste**, or press **Ctrl + V**.
   - Use **Paste Special** for more options like values-only or formatting-only paste.
3. **Keyboard Shortcuts**:
   - **Ctrl + C** (Copy), **Ctrl + X** (Cut), **Ctrl + V** (Paste).

Cutting and Pasting Data:

1. **Cutting**:

- To move data from one cell to another, use the **Cut** command. Select the cell or range of cells you want to move, then right-click and choose **Cut**, or press **Ctrl + X**.
2. **Pasting**:
   - Select the destination where you want the cut data to appear and paste it using **Ctrl + V** or right-click and select **Paste**.
3. **Paste Special**:
   - After cutting, you can use the **Paste Special** option to paste only specific aspects of the copied data, such as values, formulas, or formatting.

Filling Data:

1. **AutoFill**:
   - AutoFill is a tool that allows you to quickly copy data across a range of cells. It's especially useful when you want to fill numbers or text that follow a pattern.
   - **How to Use**:
     - Select a cell with data (e.g., the number 1 in cell A1).
     - Hover your mouse over the **bottom-right corner** of the cell until the cursor changes to a small **black cross**.
     - Drag the fill handle (the black cross) across the range of cells where you want to copy the data.
     - Release the mouse button, and Excel will fill in the cells based on the pattern or series (e.g., 1, 2, 3, 4).

2. **Flash Fill**:
   - Flash Fill is an intelligent feature that automatically fills in data based on patterns it detects as you type.
   - **How to Use**:
     - Start typing the desired pattern in a cell.
     - After typing the first few characters, press **Ctrl + E** to activate Flash Fill.
     - Excel will automatically fill the rest of the column based on the pattern you began typing.

Using Autofill and Flash Fill for Efficiency

Autofill:

1. **Using AutoFill for Numbers, Dates, and Text**:

- Autofill works with a variety of patterns, including numbers (1, 2, 3...), dates (Jan 1, Jan 2, Jan 3...), and text (January, February, March...).
- If you want to fill a series of numbers or dates, select the starting cell, drag the fill handle, and Excel will continue the series.

2. **Custom Lists**:
   - Excel also allows you to create your own lists for AutoFill (e.g., days of the week, months of the year, etc.). You can define a custom list under **File → Options → Advanced → Edit Custom Lists**.

3. **Using AutoFill with Formulas**:
   - AutoFill can also copy formulas across cells. If your formula contains relative references (e.g., =A1+B1), the formula will adjust as it's dragged to other cells.

Flash Fill:

1. **What Flash Fill Does**:
   - Flash Fill automatically fills in your data based on the patterns you start typing. For example, if you are splitting names from a full name (e.g., "John Smith" into "John" and "Smith"), Flash Fill detects the pattern and continues it for the rest of the column.

2. **How to Use Flash Fill**:
   - Start typing the pattern in the first few cells.
   - After a few characters, press **Ctrl + E** or go to the **Data** tab and click on **Flash Fill**.
   - Excel will fill the remaining cells with data based on the pattern you've established.

3. **When to Use**:

- o Flash Fill is ideal for tasks like formatting phone numbers, splitting full names, converting text to uppercase, or extracting specific parts of data.

Understanding Rows, Columns, and Cell References

Understanding how Excel organizes data in rows, columns, and cells is crucial for navigating your worksheets efficiently.

Rows and Columns:

1. **Rows**:
   - o Rows are horizontal lines in the worksheet, labeled with numbers (1, 2, 3, etc.).
   - o Each row can hold a set of data for one entity or record.
2. **Columns**:
   - o Columns are vertical stacks of cells, labeled with letters (A, B, C, etc.).
   - o Columns are used to organize data into categories (e.g., names, dates, amounts, etc.).
3. **Cell Reference**:
   - o A cell is identified by its **column letter** and **row number** (e.g., **A1**, **B2**, etc.).
   - o When you enter data or a formula into a cell, you reference the cell by its address (e.g., in a formula, you might write **=A1+B1** to add the values of cells A1 and B1).

Types of Cell References:

1. **Relative References**:
   - Default in Excel (e.g., **A1**). When you copy a formula with relative references, the cell references will change based on the position where the formula is pasted.
2. **Absolute References**:
   - Represented by dollar signs (e.g., **$A$1**). When you copy a formula with absolute references, the reference does not change.
3. **Mixed References**:
   - These combine both relative and absolute references (e.g., **$A1** or **A$1**). The row or column stays fixed depending on the placement of the dollar sign.

Pro Tips for Beginners:

- **Ctrl + D**: Fill the selected range with the data from the cell above.
- **Ctrl + R**: Fill the selected range with the data from the cell to the left.
- **Use Flash Fill for Quick Formatting**: Flash Fill is excellent for splitting and combining text, correcting capitalization, and much more.

Chapter 4. Formatting Basics

Formatting Text, Numbers, and Dates in Cells

Proper formatting of text, numbers, and dates in Excel is essential for creating a clean, readable, and professional-looking workbook. Here's how to format each type of data:

Formatting Text:

1. **Changing Font Style, Size, and Color**:
    - Select the cell or range of cells with text.
    - Go to the **Home** tab and use the **Font** group to adjust the font style (e.g., Arial, Times New Roman), font size, and font color.

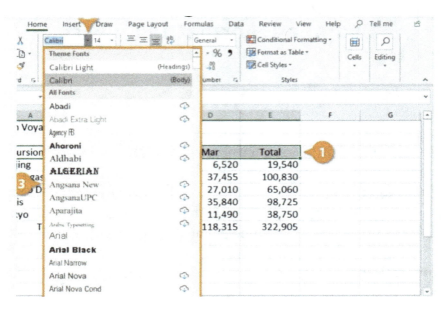

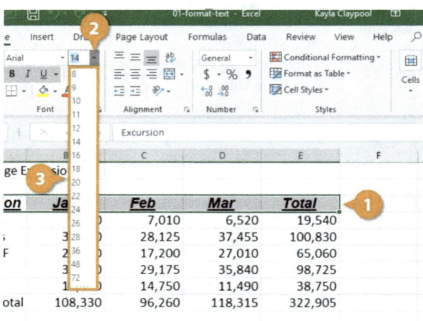

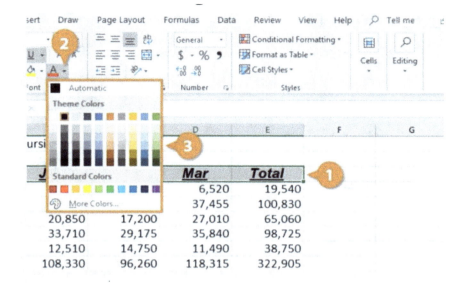

- For **bold**, **italic**, or **underline**, use the respective buttons (B, I, U).

2. **Text Alignment**:
   - You can adjust the alignment of text in a cell (left, center, or right) using the **Alignment** group in the **Home** tab.
   - For more advanced alignment, use the **Orientation** button to rotate text or adjust its vertical alignment.

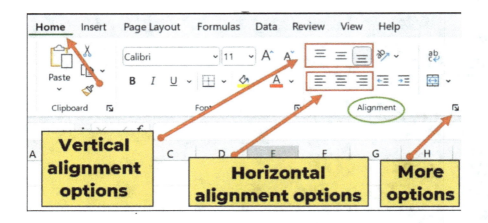

3. **Wrap Text**:
   - If you have long text in a cell that doesn't fit, select the cell, go to the **Home** tab, and click **Wrap Text**. This will make the text flow to the next line within the same cell.

Formatting Numbers:

1. **Number Formatting**:
   - Select the cell or range containing numbers.
   - Go to the **Home** tab and in the **Number** group, you can choose various formats like **Currency**, **Percentage**, **Number** (with decimal places), **Scientific**, etc.
   - For more customization, click on the **Number Format** dropdown and choose **More Number Formats** to access additional options, such as custom decimal places or adding currency symbols.
2. **Using the Increase/Decrease Decimal**:

- To control the number of decimal places shown, select the cells with numbers and use the **Increase Decimal** or **Decrease Decimal** buttons in the **Home** tab's **Number** group.

Formatting Dates:

1. **Date Format**:
   - Select the cells with dates and go to the **Home** tab.
   - Under the **Number** group, click the drop-down to select **Short Date** or **Long Date**.
   - To customize the date format, click **More Number Formats**, then select **Date** to pick from a range of predefined date formats.
2. **Changing Date Display**:
   - If you want to display the date in a different format (e.g., day-month-year, month-day-year), select the date cells, click **Format Cells**, then go to the **Number** tab and choose **Custom**. From here, you can enter a custom date format, like **DD-MM-YYYY**.

Adjusting Column Width and Row Height

To make sure your data fits neatly within cells and is easy to read, you may need to adjust the width of columns and the height of rows. Here's how to do it:

Adjusting Column Width:

1. **Manual Adjustment**:

- Hover your mouse over the boundary between two column headings (e.g., between column **A** and **B**) until the cursor turns into a double-headed arrow.
- Click and drag the boundary left or right to adjust the column width.

2. **AutoFit Column Width**:
   - To automatically adjust the column width based on the longest piece of data in that column, double-click the boundary between two column headings, or select the column(s) and go to the **Home** tab → **Cells** group → **Format** → **AutoFit Column Width**.

3. **Set a Specific Width**:
   - Select the column(s) you want to resize, right-click, and choose **Column Width**.
   - Enter a number (e.g., 15) to specify the exact width in characters.

Adjusting Row Height:

1. **Manual Adjustment**:
   - Hover your mouse over the boundary between two row numbers (e.g., between row **1** and **2**) until the cursor turns into a double-headed arrow.
   - Click and drag the boundary up or down to adjust the row height.

2. **AutoFit Row Height**:
   - To automatically adjust the row height based on the tallest item in the row, double-click the boundary between two row numbers, or select the row(s) and go to the **Home** tab → **Cells** group → **Format** → **AutoFit Row Height**.

3. **Set a Specific Height**:
    - Select the row(s) you want to resize, right-click, and choose **Row Height**.
    - Enter a number (e.g., 20) to set the exact height.

Applying Cell Borders, Shading, and Styles

Cell borders, shading, and styles enhance the visual appeal of your data, making it easier to interpret. Here's how to apply these formatting options:

Applying Cell Borders:

1. **Basic Borders**:
    - Select the cell or range of cells where you want to apply borders.
    - Go to the **Home** tab and in the **Font** group, click on the **Borders** dropdown.
    - Choose from the predefined options, such as **Bottom Border**, **Top Border**, **All Borders**, etc.
2. **Custom Borders**:
    - To customize borders, click **More Borders** at the bottom of the **Borders** dropdown menu.
    - A **Format Cells** window will open where you can adjust the border's line style, color, and position (e.g., thick outer borders, dashed lines, etc.).

Applying Cell Shading (Background Color):

1. **Adding Shading**:

- Select the cell(s) you want to shade.
- In the **Home** tab, in the **Font** group, click on the **Fill Color** bucket icon.
- Choose a color from the palette or click **More Colors** for additional options.

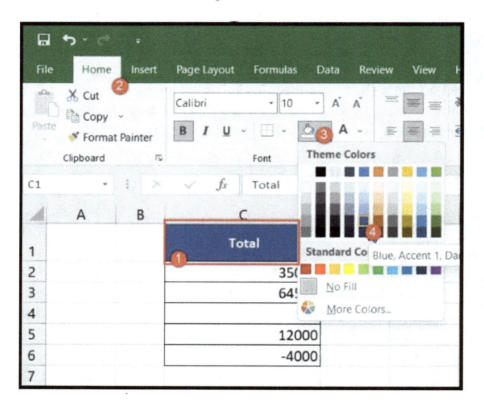

2. **Shading Multiple Cells**:
   - To apply shading to an entire row or column, select the range of cells and follow the same steps as above.

Using Cell Styles:

1. **Predefined Styles**:
   - Excel offers a variety of built-in cell styles that quickly apply combinations of formatting (font, borders, shading) to selected cells.
   - Select the cell(s) and go to the **Home** tab → **Styles** group, then click on **Cell Styles**.
   - Choose a style from the available options such as **Good, Bad, and Neutral**, **Data & Model**, or **Title**.

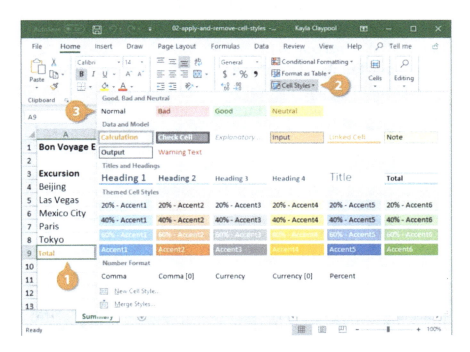

2. **Customizing Styles**:
   - To create your own custom style, click **New Cell Style** at the bottom of the **Cell Styles** gallery. In the **Style**

dialog box, you can define specific formatting settings for the style (e.g., font, borders, number format, etc.).

Pro Tips for Beginners:

- **Quick Format Shortcut**: To quickly apply bold, italic, or underline formatting, use the keyboard shortcuts **Ctrl + B**, **Ctrl + I**, and **Ctrl + U**.
- **Speeding Up Border Application**: To apply borders faster, select a range of cells and press **Ctrl + 1** to open the Format Cells dialog, then go to the **Borders** tab.
- **Conditional Formatting**: Excel also lets you apply formatting automatically based on cell values. Use **Conditional Formatting** from the **Home** tab to highlight cells, change font colors, or apply data bars based on specific criteria (e.g., highlighting sales over a certain amount).

Chapter 5. Introduction to Formulas and Functions

Formulas and functions are some of the most powerful features of Excel, allowing you to automate calculations, analyze data, and perform complex tasks with ease. In this section, we will cover the basics of using formulas and functions in Excel.

Understanding Formulas and How to Enter Them

A **formula** in Excel is an expression that calculates the value of a cell. It starts with an equal sign (=), followed by the formula logic.

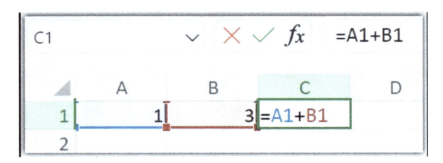

Steps to Enter a Formula:

1. **Select a Cell**:
    o Click on the cell where you want to display the result.

2. **Type the Formula**:
   - ○ Begin by typing an equal sign (=) to indicate that you are entering a formula. For example, to add two numbers, type =5+3.
3. **Press Enter**:
   - ○ After entering the formula, press **Enter**. Excel will calculate the result and display it in the cell.

Example:

- **Basic Addition**: In cell A1, type =5+3. Press **Enter**. The result will be 8.

Formulas can include numbers, cell references, and even other formulas.

Basic Arithmetic Operations (Addition, Subtraction, Multiplication, Division)

Excel performs basic arithmetic operations using operators. These operators can be combined to create more complex formulas.

Addition (+):

- To add two numbers, use the plus sign (+).
- **Example**: =5+3 will return 8.

Subtraction (-):

- To subtract one number from another, use the minus sign (-).
- **Example**: =10-4 will return 6.

Multiplication (*):

- To multiply two numbers, use the asterisk (*).
- **Example**: =6*7 will return 42.

Division (/)

- To divide one number by another, use the slash (/).
- **Example**: =20/4 will return 5.

Order of Operations (PEMDAS):

Excel follows the order of operations (Parentheses, Exponents, Multiplication and Division, Addition and Subtraction, or PEMDAS).

- For example, =5 + 3 * 2 will return 11, not 16, because multiplication is done before addition.

To enforce a particular order, use parentheses. For instance, =(5 + 3) * 2 will return 16.

Essential Functions for Beginners: SUM, AVERAGE, COUNT, MAX, MIN

Functions are predefined formulas in Excel that perform specific calculations. Here are five basic functions that every beginner should know:

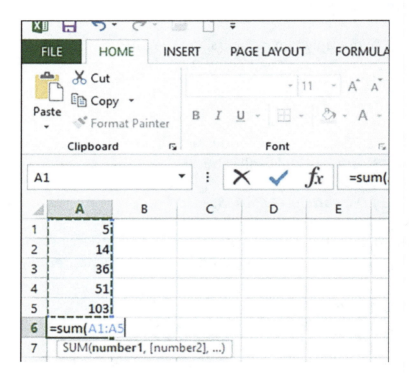

1. SUM Function:

- **Purpose**: Adds up a range of numbers.
- **Syntax**: =SUM(number1, number2, ...)

Steps:

- To add a series of numbers, type =SUM(A1:A5), where A1:A5 is the range of cells you want to add.

Example:

- If you have values in cells A1 to A5 (e.g., 5, 10, 15, 20, and 25), the formula =SUM(A1:A5) will return 75.

2. AVERAGE Function:

- **Purpose**: Calculates the average (mean) of a range of numbers.
- **Syntax**: =AVERAGE(number1, number2, ...)

Steps:

- To calculate the average, use =AVERAGE(B1:B5), where B1:B5 is the range of cells.

Example:

- If the values in cells B1 to B5 are 10, 20, 30, 40, and 50, =AVERAGE(B1:B5) will return 30.

3. COUNT Function:

- **Purpose**: Counts the number of cells that contain numbers in a given range.
- **Syntax**: =COUNT(range)

Steps:

- To count how many cells in a range contain numbers, use =COUNT(C1:C6).

Example:

- If C1 to C6 contains 2, 4, 5, "apple", 6, "banana", the formula =COUNT(C1:C6) will return 4 because there are 4 numeric values.

4. MAX Function:

- **Purpose**: Finds the largest number in a range of cells.
- **Syntax**: =MAX(number1, number2, ...)

Steps:

- To find the highest value in a range, use =MAX(D1:D10).

Example:

- If the values in D1 to D10 are 4, 2, 8, 15, 9, 22, 13, =MAX(D1:D10) will return 22.

5. MIN Function:

- **Purpose**: Finds the smallest number in a range of cells.
- **Syntax**: =MIN(number1, number2, ...)

Steps:

- To find the smallest value in a range, use =MIN(E1:E8).

Example:

- If the values in E1 to E8 are 45, 30, 12, 60, 8, 39, =MIN(E1:E8)
  will return 8.

Understanding Relative, Absolute, and Mixed References

In Excel, references are the addresses of cells that appear in formulas. There are three types of references:

1. Relative References:

- **Definition**: A relative reference changes when you copy a formula from one cell to another. This is the default reference type in Excel.

Example:

- If you enter =A1+B1 in cell C1, and then copy that formula to C2, Excel will automatically adjust the references to =A2+B2.

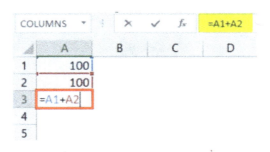

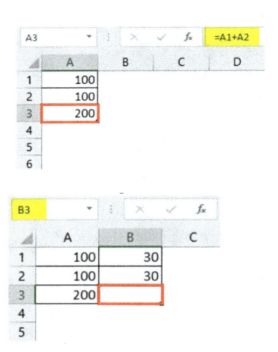

Alternatively, you can decide to copy from the cell A3 and paste it in cell B3 instead of dragging from A3 to B3.

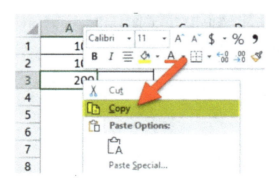

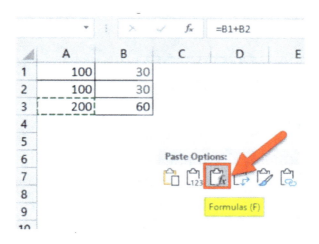

2. Absolute References:

- **Definition**: An absolute reference does not change when you copy a formula to another cell. This is indicated by the use of dollar signs ($).

Steps:

- To make a reference absolute, place dollar signs in front of the column and row number. For example, =$A$1+$B$1.

Example:

- If you copy =$A$1+$B$1 from C1 to C2, the reference will remain =$A$1+$B$1.

3. Mixed References:

- **Definition**: A mixed reference is a combination of relative and absolute references. In this case, either the row or the column is fixed while the other is relative.

Steps:

- **Absolute Row**: $A1 (column is relative, but row is fixed).
- **Absolute Column**: A$1 (row is relative, but column is fixed).

Example:

- If you copy =$A1+B$1 from cell C1 to C2, the formula becomes =$A2+B$1. Here, the row in A changes, but the row in B stays the same.

Pro Tips for Beginners:

- **Quick Fill**: Use the **Fill Handle** (small square at the bottom-right corner of a cell) to drag a formula down or across to adjacent cells.
- **Use Functions with Arguments**: Many functions like SUM and AVERAGE accept arguments (ranges or numbers). Make

sure you separate the arguments with commas (e.g., =SUM(A1:A5, B1:B5)).

- **Formula Auditing**: Use the **Formulas** tab to enable **Show Formulas**, **Trace Precedents**, or **Trace Dependents** to better understand how formulas are connected across cells.

Chapter 6. Organizing and Managing Data

Efficiently organizing and managing data is key to maximizing the power of Excel. This section covers essential features to sort, filter, and validate data, ensuring you can work with large datasets effectively and avoid common mistakes.

Sorting and Filtering Data

Sorting and filtering are essential techniques for organizing data in Excel, allowing you to quickly find what you need and present your data logically.

Sorting Data:

Sorting allows you to arrange your data in a specified order—either alphabetically, numerically, or by date.

Steps to Sort Data:

1. **Select the Range**:
   o Click on a cell within the range you want to sort.
2. **Go to the Data Tab**:
   o Click on the **Data** tab in the Ribbon.
3. **Choose Sort Options**:

- o To sort in ascending order (A-Z or smallest to largest), click the **Sort A to Z** button.
- o To sort in descending order (Z-A or largest to smallest), click the **Sort Z to A** button.

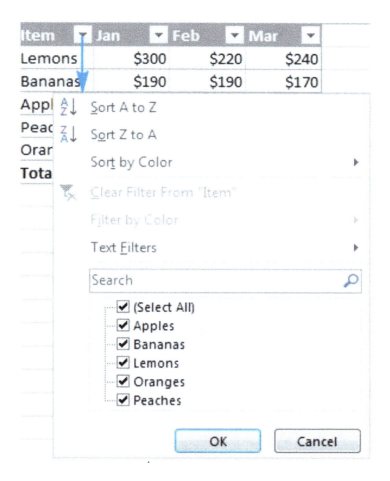

4. **Customize Sort**:
   - o Click on **Sort** for more advanced options:
     - ▪ Choose the column to sort by.

- Choose whether to sort by values, cell color, font color, or cell icon.
- Specify whether you want to sort in ascending or descending order.

Example:

- If you have a list of employee names in Column A and their ages in Column B, you can sort the names alphabetically or sort by age, either from youngest to oldest or vice versa.

Filtering Data:

Filtering allows you to display only the rows that meet specific criteria, hiding the rest.

Steps to Filter Data:

1. **Select Your Data**:
   - Click on any cell within your data range.
2. **Activate the Filter**:
   - Click on the **Data** tab, then click **Filter**. This will add a dropdown arrow to each column header.
3. **Apply the Filter**:
   - Click the dropdown arrow in the column you want to filter.
   - Choose specific criteria (e.g., text, numbers, dates).
   - You can filter by specific values, conditions, or search for certain items.

Example:

- If you have a dataset with columns for "City" and "Sales," you can filter to only show the rows where the "City" is "New York" or where "Sales" exceed $1000.

Advanced Filter Options:

- Use the **Text Filters** and **Number Filters** options in the dropdown to filter by conditions like "contains," "begins with," or "greater than."

Creating and Formatting Tables

Tables are a powerful feature in Excel that help organize and structure your data for better readability and easier management.

Creating a Table:

To turn a range of data into a table, follow these steps:

Steps to Create a Table:

1. **Select the Data**:
   o Highlight the range of cells you want to convert into a table (including headers).
2. **Insert a Table**:
   o Go to the **Insert** tab on the Ribbon.
   o Click on the **Table** button.
3. **Confirm the Range**:

- In the **Create Table** dialog box, check that the correct range is selected. Ensure the "My table has headers" box is checked if your data has column headers.
4. **Click OK**:
   - Click **OK** to create the table.

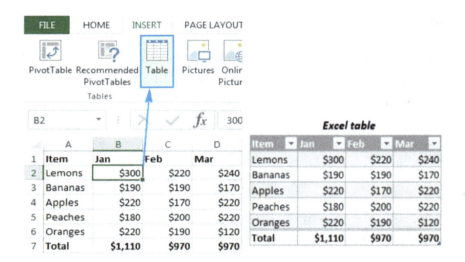

Formatting the Table:

Once you've created your table, Excel automatically applies a default style. You can modify the table style to suit your preferences.

Steps to Format the Table:

1. **Table Tools**:
   - With the table selected, the **Table Tools Design** tab will appear on the Ribbon.
2. **Choose a Table Style**:
   - Select a pre-built table style from the **Table Styles** gallery.

3. **Customize Table Options**:
   o Modify the table design by checking options like **Banded Rows**, **First Column**, or **Last Column**.

Table Features:

- **AutoFill**: As you add data to a table, Excel automatically extends formulas, formats, and styles.
- **Sorting and Filtering**: Each column header includes filter buttons for sorting and filtering the table's data.
- **Structured References**: When working within a table, Excel uses structured references, like Table1[Sales], instead of cell references.

Example:

- If you have a sales report, convert your data to a table to easily filter sales by region or salesperson.

Using Data Validation (Dropdown Lists and Restrictions)

Data validation helps prevent errors and ensures the data entered into a cell meets certain criteria. You can use it to restrict data entry, create dropdown lists, or ensure that only specific types of data are entered.

Creating a Dropdown List:

A dropdown list lets users select a value from a predefined list, ensuring data consistency and reducing errors.

Steps to Create a Dropdown List:

1. **Select the Cell(s)**:
   - Click on the cell or range where you want the dropdown list.
2. **Go to the Data Tab**:
   - Click the **Data** tab on the Ribbon.
   - Select **Data Validation** from the **Data Tools** group.
3. **Set Data Validation Criteria**:
   - In the **Data Validation** dialog box, go to the **Settings** tab.
   - Under **Allow**, select **List** from the dropdown.
4. **Enter the List Items**:
   - In the **Source** box, type the items for your list, separated by commas (e.g., "Red, Green, Blue").
   - Alternatively, select a range of cells that contain the list items.
5. **Click OK**:
   - After clicking **OK**, the selected cell(s) will have a dropdown arrow.

Example:

- Create a dropdown list for selecting a department (e.g., "Sales," "Marketing," "HR") in an employee directory.

Setting Data Validation Criteria:

You can restrict what users can enter into a cell by setting criteria.

Steps to Set Restrictions:

1. **Select the Cell(s)**:
    o   Select the range of cells where you want to apply data validation.
2. **Open Data Validation**:
    o   Go to the **Data** tab and click **Data Validation**.
3. **Set Validation Criteria**:
    o   Under the **Settings** tab, select the type of data allowed:
        ▪   **Whole Number**: Restrict entry to whole numbers (e.g., =10).
        ▪   **Decimal**: Allow decimal numbers.
        ▪   **Date**: Restrict to dates within a specified range.
        ▪   **Text Length**: Limit the number of characters entered.
4. **Set Error Alerts**:
    o   Under the **Error Alert** tab, customize the message that appears when users enter invalid data.

Example:

- Set a validation to only allow dates within the current year or restrict the age to numbers between 18 and 65.

Pro Tips for Managing Data:

- **Remove Duplicates**: To eliminate duplicate entries in a range, go to **Data > Remove Duplicates**.

- **Named Ranges**: Give ranges a name (e.g., "SalesData") to make formulas and references easier to manage.
- **Conditional Formatting**: Use **Conditional Formatting** to highlight cells based on specific criteria (e.g., highlight sales greater than $1000).

Chapter 7. Introduction to Data Visualization

Data visualization is a powerful tool in Excel that helps you present complex data in a visually appealing and easy-to-understand format. This chapter covers how to create charts, customize chart elements, and use conditional formatting to enhance data presentation.

Creating Charts (Bar, Line, Pie, and Column Charts)

Charts are one of the best ways to summarize and present data in Excel. They help make your data visually accessible, enabling you to spot trends and patterns quickly. This section will guide you through creating common types of charts.

Steps to Create a Chart:

1. **Select Your Data**:
    o   Highlight the data you want to chart, including the headers (e.g., labels or categories).

	A	B	C	D	E
1	Month	Bears	Dolphins	Whales	
2	Jan	8	150	80	
3	Feb	54	77	54	
4	Mar	93	32	100	
5	Apr	116	11	76	
6	May	137	6	93	
7	Jun	184	1	72	
8					

2. **Insert a Chart**:
   - Go to the **Insert** tab in the Ribbon.
   - In the **Charts** group, choose the type of chart you want to create. You can select from options like **Column, Bar, Line, Pie, Area**, and more.
3. **Choose a Chart Style**:
   - For basic charts, you can click on the chart type (e.g., **Clustered Column**) to insert it.
   - For more advanced charts, you can click the **Insert Statistical Chart** or **Insert Other Charts** dropdown to access specialized charts like **Waterfall, Radar**, or **Funnel**.

Types of Charts:

1. **Bar and Column Charts**:
   - **Bar charts** are useful for comparing categories side by side.

- ○ **Column charts** are similar but display data vertically.

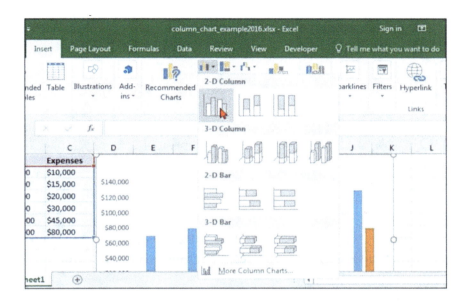

When to Use: To compare values across categories, such as sales by product or revenue by month.

2. **Line Charts**:
   - ○ Line charts are excellent for showing trends over time.

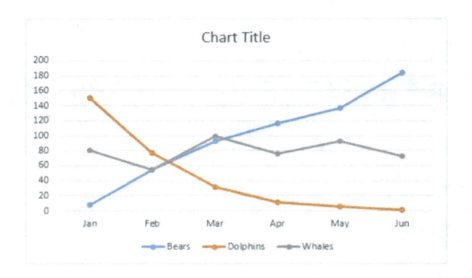

When to Use: To visualize changes over time, such as monthly sales, stock prices, or temperature variations.

3. **Pie Charts**:
   o Pie charts represent parts of a whole, showing how individual segments contribute to the total.

   When to Use: To display proportions, such as market share or budget allocation.

Example:

- You have sales data for four quarters of the year and want to visualize the total sales trend. A **line chart** would help you see the increase or decrease in sales over time.

Customizing Chart Elements (Titles, Legends, and Labels)

Once you've created a chart, customizing it can make the information clearer and more engaging. You can modify chart elements like titles, axis labels, legends, and data labels to improve readability.

Adding and Customizing Chart Titles:

1. **Click on the Chart**:
   - ○ Select your chart.
2. **Add a Chart Title**:
   - ○ If the chart title isn't displayed, click on the **Chart Elements** button (a plus sign next to the chart).
   - ○ Check **Chart Title**, and a title will appear at the top of the chart.
3. **Edit the Title**:
   - ○ Double-click the title box to edit it and enter a more descriptive title (e.g., "Quarterly Sales Comparison").

Modifying Legends and Labels:

1. **Change the Legend**:
   - ○ Click on the **Chart Elements** button, then check **Legend** to display it. The legend explains what the data series represent.
   - ○ Click on the legend to move it to a different position or format it (e.g., changing the font style).

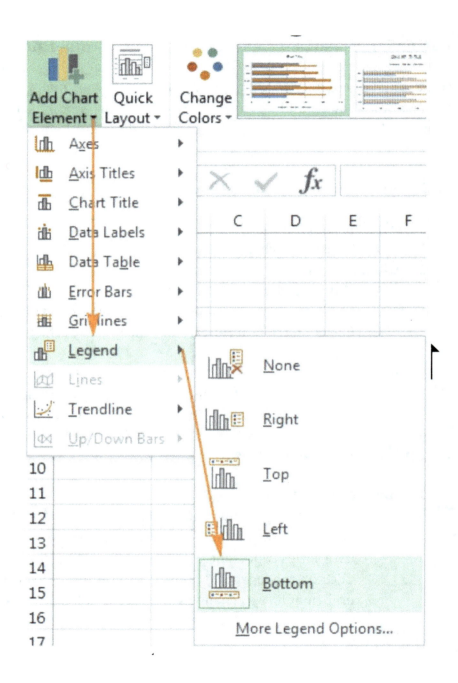

Another way to move the legend is to double-click on it in the chart, and then choose the desired legend position on the *Format Legend* pane under *Legend Options*.

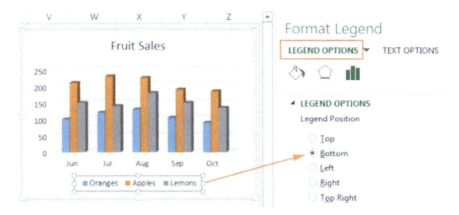

2. **Add Data Labels**:
   o Use **Data Labels** to show the exact value of each data point on the chart. To add them, click on the **Chart Elements** button and select **Data Labels**.
   o You can choose from options such as **Inside End**, **Outside End**, or **Center** for label positioning.

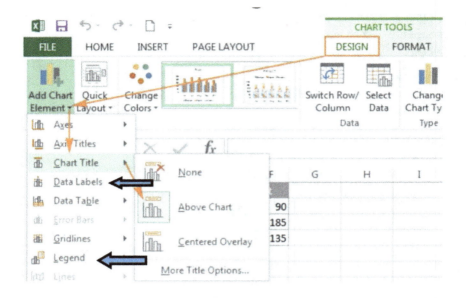

Customizing Axis Labels:

1. **Edit Axis Titles**:
   o To make it clear what each axis represents, add axis titles by clicking the **Chart Elements** button and selecting **Axis Titles**.
   o Label the X-axis (horizontal) and Y-axis (vertical) with appropriate descriptions, such as "Months" or "Sales ($)."

2. **Modify Axis Scale**:
   o Right-click on the axis and select **Format Axis** to adjust the range, intervals, and other settings. For instance, you can change the axis minimum and maximum values to better display data.

Using Conditional Formatting for Visual Cues

Conditional formatting is a powerful tool in Excel that changes the appearance of cells based on their values, helping to draw attention to important data points. It's a great way to visually highlight trends, patterns, or outliers in your data.

Steps to Apply Conditional Formatting:

1. **Select the Range**:
    o   Highlight the cells or range of data that you want to apply conditional formatting to.
2. **Go to the Home Tab**:
    o   On the **Home** tab, click on the **Conditional Formatting** dropdown in the **Styles** group.
3. **Choose a Formatting Rule**:
    o   You can choose from a variety of options, including:
        ▪   **Highlight Cell Rules**: Highlight cells that meet specific conditions, such as greater than, less than, or equal to a certain number.
        ▪   **Top/Bottom Rules**: Highlight the highest or lowest values in a range.
        ▪   **Data Bars, Color Scales, and Icon Sets**: These options add visual elements to your data, such as color gradients, bars, or icons.

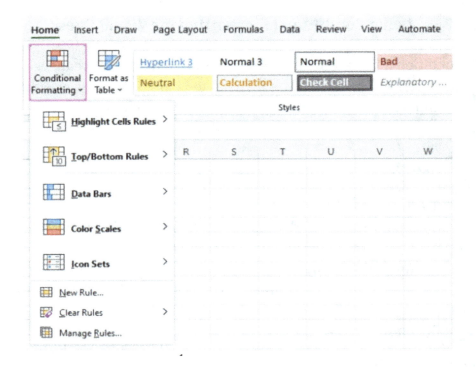

4. **Customize the Rule**:
   o Once you've selected a rule, you can customize the formatting, such as changing colors or the icon style.

Example:

- Highlight the top 10 highest sales figures in a column by selecting **Top/Bottom Rules** and choosing **Top 10 Items**. Excel will automatically highlight the highest values with a specified color.

Types of Conditional Formatting:

1. **Highlighting Values**:

- o Highlight cells that are greater than a specific value, contain certain text, or are duplicates.
2. **Data Bars**:
   - o Data bars visually represent the magnitude of values in the cells, giving a quick indication of relative size.
3. **Color Scales**:
   - o Color scales apply a gradient of colors to your data, which helps to visually compare different values within the range (e.g., red to green, with red indicating lower values and green representing higher values).
4. **Icon Sets**:
   - o Icon sets add icons (such as arrows, traffic lights, or stars) to cells based on the values. For example, a green arrow can represent a positive change, while a red arrow can represent a decrease.

Example of Conditional Formatting:

- If you have a sales performance table, you could apply conditional formatting to show a **red-green color scale** where low values are shaded red and high values are shaded green. This visually represents high and low performers.

Pro Tips for Data Visualization:

- **Chart Recommendations**: Excel provides recommended charts based on your data. Click **Insert** > **Recommended**

Charts to automatically see what chart type would work best.

- **Dynamic Charts with Pivot Tables**: Combine PivotTables and PivotCharts for interactive data analysis and visualizations. PivotCharts can be updated dynamically as your data changes.
- **Chart Design**: Keep your charts simple and uncluttered. Too many elements can confuse the viewer and make the data hard to read.

Chapter 8. Basic Data Analysis Tools

Excel provides powerful tools for analyzing data, and two of the most widely used features are **PivotTables** and **PivotCharts**. These tools allow you to summarize, explore, and visualize large datasets in an interactive and meaningful way. Additionally, **Slicers** enable you to filter your data dynamically for better analysis. This chapter will cover the basics of using these data analysis tools.

Introduction to PivotTables and PivotCharts

PivotTables and PivotCharts are Excel's most advanced tools for data summarization and analysis. They allow you to quickly summarize and explore complex data by organizing it into rows and columns. PivotTables work with structured data to give you insight into trends, patterns, and relationships.

What is a PivotTable?

A **PivotTable** is an interactive table that automatically sorts, organizes, and summarizes your data in a new format. It allows you to group, filter, and calculate data dynamically, making it easier to analyze and draw insights.

	A	B	C	D
1	**Product**	**Reseller**	**Month**	**Sales**
2	Cherries	John	Oct	$250
3	Bananas	Mike	Nov	$200
4	Apples	Pete	Oct	$180
5	Oranges	Mike	Nov	$400
6	Bananas	Sally	Oct	$250
7	Apples	Mike	Oct	$120
8	Cherries	Sally	Sep	$330
9	Apples	Pete	Oct	$110
10	Cherries	Mike	Sep	$250

Pivot Table 1

Sales	Sep	Oct	Nov	Total
Apples	250	590		840
John		180		180
Mike		120		120
Pete		290		290
Sally	250			250
Bananas		430	600	1030
John			400	400
Mike			200	200
Pete		180		180
Sally		250		250
Cherries	580	910		1490
John		250		250
Mike	250	330		580
Pete		330		330
Sally	330			330
Oranges		120	720	840
John		120		120
Mike			400	400
Pete		120		120
Sally			200	200
Total	830	2050	1320	4200

Pivot Table 2

Month (All)

Sales	Product				
Reseller	Apples	Bananas	Cherries	Oranges	Total
John	$180	$400	$250	$120	$950
Mike	$120	$200	$580	$400	$1,300
Pete	$290	$180	$330	$120	$920
Sally	$250	$250	$330	$200	$1,030
Total	$840	$1,030	$1,490	$840	$4,200

Pivot Table 3

Product (All)

Sales	Month			
Reseller	Sep	Oct	Nov	Total
John		$430	$520	$950
Mike	$250	$450	$600	$1,300
Pete		$920		$920
Sally	$580	$250	$200	$1,030
Total	$830	$2,050	$1,320	$4,200

166

What is a PivotChart?

A **PivotChart** is a graphical representation of the data summarized in a PivotTable. PivotCharts update automatically as the underlying PivotTable data changes, providing a visual element to your data analysis.

Steps to Create a PivotTable

1. **Select Your Data**:
   - Before creating a PivotTable, make sure your data is organized in a tabular format, with column headers at the top and no blank rows or columns within the dataset.
2. **Insert a PivotTable**:
   - Highlight the range of data you want to analyze.
   - Go to the **Insert** tab on the Ribbon.
   - In the **Tables** group, click on **PivotTable**.

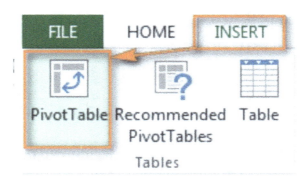

o Excel will display a dialog box asking if you want to create the PivotTable in a new worksheet or an existing worksheet. Choose your preferred option.

3. **Choose the Data Source**:
  o If your data is in a different workbook, click on **Use an External Data Source**.
  o If the data is in the current workbook, make sure the correct range is selected.

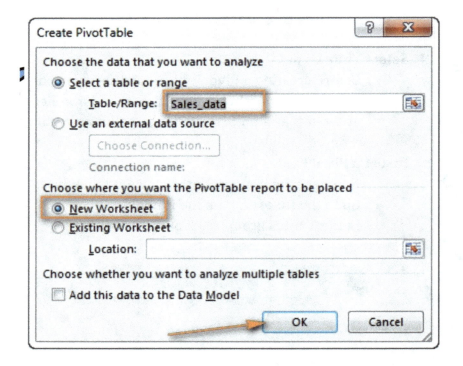

4. **Build the PivotTable**:
  o After clicking **OK**, the **PivotTable Field List** pane will appear. You'll see a list of the column headers from your data.

- Drag and drop fields into the four areas of the PivotTable Field List:
  - **Rows**: Data that you want to group by.
  - **Columns**: Data that will appear across the top of the PivotTable.
  - **Values**: The data you want to summarize (e.g., sums, counts, averages).
  - **Filters**: Data you want to use to filter the PivotTable results.

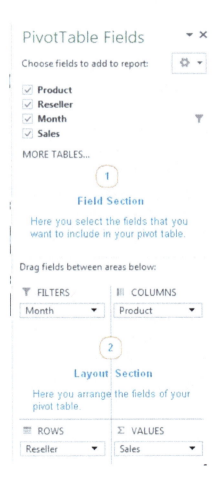

Grouping and Summarizing Data with PivotTables

One of the key strengths of PivotTables is the ability to group data and summarize it in different ways. You can use them to group data by categories, calculate sums and averages, or apply custom grouping.

Steps to Group Data in a PivotTable:

1. **Group by Date**:
   o If you have date data (e.g., sales by date), Excel can automatically group this data into years, months, quarters, etc. Right-click on any date value in the PivotTable, choose **Group**, and select how you want to group the data (e.g., by month or year).
2. **Group by Numeric Ranges**:
   o If you have numerical data and want to group it into ranges (e.g., income brackets), right-click a number in the PivotTable, select **Group**, and choose the number range you want to create.
3. **Summarize Data**:
   o By default, PivotTables will sum numeric data. However, you can change this by clicking on a value field in the PivotTable, selecting **Value Field Settings**, and choosing a different summary function (e.g., Average, Count, Max, Min).

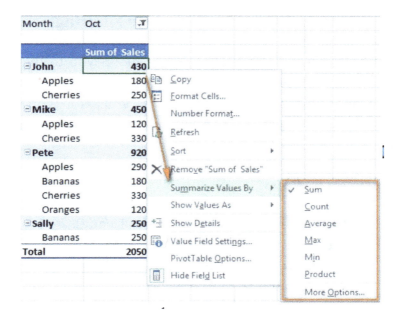

4. **Multiple Groupings**:

   o You can add multiple fields to the **Rows** and **Columns**
   areas to create multi-level groupings. For example,
   you can group sales data by both **Product Category**
   and **Region**.

Example:

- You have sales data with the columns **Date**, **Product**, and
  Amount. A PivotTable can group the data by month and
  show the total sales amount for each month.

Using Slicers for Interactive Filtering

A **Slicer** is a powerful tool in Excel that allows you to filter your PivotTable or PivotChart interactively. Slicers provide a user-friendly way to filter data, making it easy for you to focus on specific subsets of your data without needing to manually adjust the filter settings.

Steps to Insert a Slicer:

1. **Create a PivotTable** (if you haven't already).
2. **Insert the Slicer**:
   - Click anywhere inside the PivotTable to activate the PivotTable Tools.
   - Go to the **Insert** tab on the Ribbon.
   - Click **Slicer** in the **Filters** group.
3. **Select Fields for the Slicer**:
   - In the dialog box that appears, check the boxes next to the fields you want to use for filtering (e.g., **Product**, **Region**, **Month**).
4. **Click OK**:
   - The slicer(s) will appear as small boxes with buttons representing each filter option (e.g., Product categories or Regions).

Using the Slicer to Filter Data:

- Click the buttons in the Slicer to filter the data dynamically. You can select multiple items by holding the **Ctrl** key while clicking. To clear the filter, click the **Clear Filter** button on the Slicer.

Customizing Slicers:

1. **Resize and Move**: You can resize and move Slicers around your worksheet to organize them.
2. **Change the Style**: Right-click the Slicer and choose **Slicer Settings** to change the style, size, and layout.

Creating PivotCharts from PivotTables

A **PivotChart** is an excellent way to visually represent the data summarized in a PivotTable. PivotCharts provide an interactive chart that updates automatically as you change the PivotTable data.

Steps to Create a PivotChart:

1. **Select the PivotTable**:
   o Click anywhere inside the PivotTable to activate it.
2. **Insert a PivotChart**:
   o Go to the **Insert** tab on the Ribbon.
   o In the **Charts** group, click **PivotChart**.
3. **Choose the Chart Type**:
   o Excel will display a dialog box asking you to select the type of chart (e.g., bar, line, column). Choose a chart type that best represents your data.
4. **Customize the Chart**:
   o You can modify the chart's title, labels, legends, and colors just like any other chart in Excel.

Pro Tips for PivotTables and PivotCharts:

- **Refresh Data**: If the source data changes, right-click anywhere in the PivotTable and select **Refresh** to update the data in your PivotTable and PivotChart.
- **Multiple Consolidation Ranges**: When analyzing data from multiple sources or worksheets, use the **Multiple Consolidation Ranges** option to combine data in one PivotTable.
- **Use Slicers for Dashboards**: Combine multiple PivotTables, PivotCharts, and Slicers to create interactive data dashboards. This allows you to analyze data dynamically and from different perspectives.
- **Explore PivotTable Options**: Right-click on different areas of the PivotTable to access options like **Show Values As** to display data as percentages, ranks, or running totals.

Chapter 9. Time-Saving Tools in Excel

Excel offers several time-saving tools designed to make your workflow more efficient, especially when you're working with large amounts of data. These tools streamline repetitive tasks, automate processes, and allow you to quickly access frequently used commands. In this chapter, we'll explore **AutoSum**, **AutoComplete**, the **Quick Access Toolbar**, and **Macros**.

Using AutoSum and AutoComplete

AutoSum

The **AutoSum** tool allows you to quickly calculate sums, averages, counts, and other basic mathematical functions for a selected range of data. It's a convenient shortcut for adding formulas to your worksheet without needing to type them manually.

How to Use AutoSum:

1. **Sum Function**:
   - Select the cell where you want the result to appear.
   - Click on the **Formulas** tab in the Ribbon.
   - In the **Function Library** group, click on **AutoSum** (Σ).
   - Excel will automatically select the range of cells it thinks you want to sum. If it's correct, just press **Enter**.

- o If Excel selects the wrong range, drag the cursor to select the correct range before pressing **Enter**.
2. **Other AutoSum Functions**:
   - o After clicking **AutoSum**, you can also select other functions like **Average**, **Count**, **Max**, and **Min** by clicking the small dropdown arrow next to AutoSum.

Example:

- You have a column of sales numbers from cells A1 to A10. Place your cursor in cell A11 (below the sales data) and click the **AutoSum** button. Excel will automatically sum the data in cells A1 to A10, and you'll get the total sales value in cell A11.

AutoComplete

AutoComplete in Excel speeds up data entry by automatically filling in values based on previously typed data. This tool is especially useful when you're entering repetitive data, such as names, months, or product categories.

How to Use AutoComplete:

1. **Start Typing**: Begin typing a value in a cell. If Excel recognizes it as a previously entered value, it will suggest a match.
2. **Accept the Suggestion**: If the suggestion is correct, press **Enter** or use the **Arrow keys** to select the suggestion and press **Enter**.

3. **Disable AutoComplete**: To turn off AutoComplete, go to the **File** menu, select **Options**, click **Advanced**, and uncheck the box for **Enable AutoComplete for cell values**.

Example:

- When typing a month, like "January," Excel will suggest "January" again the next time you start typing it, allowing you to save time and ensure consistency in your data entry.

Customizing the Quick Access Toolbar

The **Quick Access Toolbar (QAT)** is a customizable toolbar that allows you to add shortcuts to your most frequently used commands. It's located at the top-left corner of the Excel window, and by adding your favorite commands to it, you can access them with just one click.

How to Customize the Quick Access Toolbar:

1. **Add Commands**:
    o   Click the small down arrow at the right end of the Quick Access Toolbar.
    o   From the dropdown menu, select **More Commands** to open the **Excel Options** dialog box.
    o   In the dialog box, you'll see a list of available commands. Select the commands you want to add to the QAT and click **Add**.
2. **Remove Commands**:

o   To remove a command from the QAT, select it in the list and click **Remove**.

3. **Change the Position**:
    o   You can choose to display the QAT above or below the Ribbon. To do this, right-click the Quick Access Toolbar and select **Show Below the Ribbon** or **Show Above the Ribbon**.

4. **Customize by Command Type**:
    o   You can add commands from the Ribbon, file-related commands (like Save or Open), or commands related to formatting, data, or charts.

Example:

- You frequently use the **Bold** formatting option. Instead of navigating through the Ribbon each time, you can add **Bold** to the QAT for easy access with just one click.

Introduction to Macros (Recording and Running)

A **Macro** is a series of actions or commands that you can record and then execute with a single click. Macros are incredibly useful for automating repetitive tasks, saving you time and effort. In Excel, macros are written in a programming language called **VBA (Visual Basic for Applications)**, but you don't need to know programming to create simple macros—Excel allows you to record your actions and convert them into a macro.

How to Record a Macro:

1. **Enable the Developer Tab**:
    o By default, the **Developer** tab isn't visible. To enable it, go to the **File** menu, select **Options**, click **Customize Ribbon**, and check the box for **Developer** in the right-hand column.
2. **Record the Macro**:
    o Click the **Developer** tab in the Ribbon.
    o In the **Code** group, click on **Record Macro**.
    o In the dialog box, give your macro a name, and choose whether to assign a shortcut key or store the macro in the current workbook or a new one.

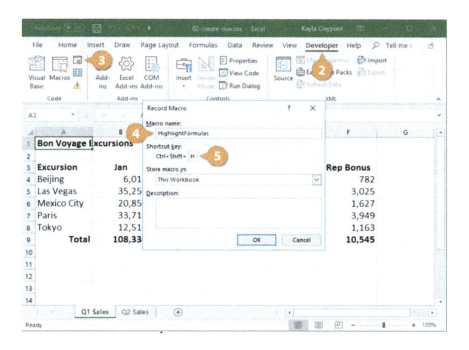

- Perform the actions you want to automate. Excel will record every step you take, including typing, formatting, or changing cell values.
- Once done, click **Stop Recording** (found in the Developer tab).

3. **Running the Macro**:
   - To run the recorded macro, press the **Macro** button in the Developer tab.

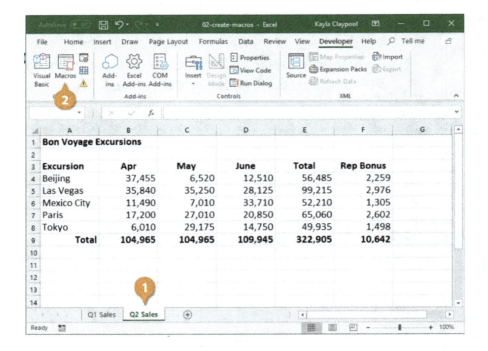

- Select the macro you want to run and click **Run**.

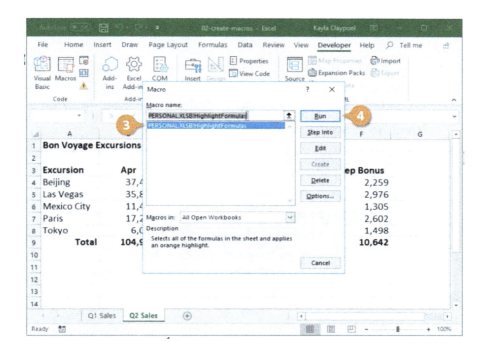

How to Assign a Macro to a Button:

1. Once your macro is recorded, you can assign it to a button on the worksheet for easy access.
2. Go to the **Developer** tab, and click on **Insert**.
3. Select **Button** from the **Form Controls** group, and draw the button on your worksheet.
4. In the dialog box that appears, select the macro you want to assign to the button.

Pro Tips for Time-Saving Tools:

- **Use Keyboard Shortcuts**: Familiarize yourself with Excel keyboard shortcuts to speed up your workflow. For example, use **Ctrl + C** to copy, **Ctrl + V** to paste, and **Ctrl + Z** to undo actions.
- **Record Complex Macros**: Even if you don't know VBA, you can use recorded macros to automate complicated tasks. For instance, if you routinely format reports in a specific way, a macro can save you significant time.
- **Macro Security**: Be cautious when running macros from unknown sources, as they can contain harmful code. Always set Excel's macro security settings to **Disable all macros with notification** to protect your data.

Chapter 10. Collaboration and Sharing in Excel

In today's collaborative work environment, Excel makes it easy to share and work together on workbooks. Whether you're working with a team, co-authoring reports, or simply ensuring that your data is secure, Excel provides several tools to manage and track changes. This chapter will cover how to **protect your worksheets and workbooks**, **track changes and add comments**, and **share workbooks online via OneDrive**.

Protecting Worksheets and Workbooks

One of the first steps in collaboration is ensuring that the right people can edit the content and that sensitive data is kept safe. Excel allows you to protect both individual worksheets and the entire workbook to prevent unauthorized changes.

How to Protect a Worksheet:

1. **Select the Worksheet**:
   - Click the tab of the worksheet you want to protect.
2. **Open the Protection Options**:
   - Go to the **Review** tab in the Ribbon.
   - Click on **Protect Sheet**.
3. **Set Protection Options**:

- In the dialog box, you can choose what users can or cannot do, such as formatting cells, inserting rows, or deleting columns.
- Enter a password if you want to restrict access to users who don't know the password (optional but highly recommended for stronger security).
- Click **OK**. If you entered a password, confirm it by typing it again.

How to Protect a Workbook:

1. **Go to the File Tab**:
   - Click on the **File** tab and choose **Info**.
2. **Choose Protect Workbook**:
   - Click on **Protect Workbook** and select **Encrypt with Password** from the dropdown.
3. **Enter a Password**:
   - Enter a password and click **OK**. Make sure to remember this password—if forgotten, it cannot be recovered.

Unprotecting a Worksheet or Workbook:

To unprotect, simply return to the **Review** tab (for worksheets) or the **File** tab (for workbooks), and enter the password to remove the protection.

Tracking Changes and Adding Comments

When collaborating with others, it's essential to track changes and maintain a record of who made those changes. Excel provides built-in tools to track modifications, highlight edits, and add comments to help clarify data.

Tracking Changes:

1. **Turn On Track Changes**:
   - Go to the **Review** tab.
   - Click on **Track Changes** (in the Changes group) and select **Highlight Changes**.
2. **Set Change Tracking Options**:
   - In the dialog box, select options like:
     - "Track changes while editing" to highlight changes.
     - "Highlight changes on screen" to show the changes in the worksheet.
     - Choose to track changes from all users or only specific users.
3. **View and Accept/Reject Changes**:
   - After changes have been made, return to **Track Changes** and select **Accept or Reject Changes** to review and finalize changes.

Adding Comments:

Adding comments is an easy way to provide additional context or ask questions about specific cells without altering the data.

1. **Insert a Comment**:

- Right-click on the cell where you want to add a comment.
- Select **New Comment** or **Insert Comment** depending on your Excel version.

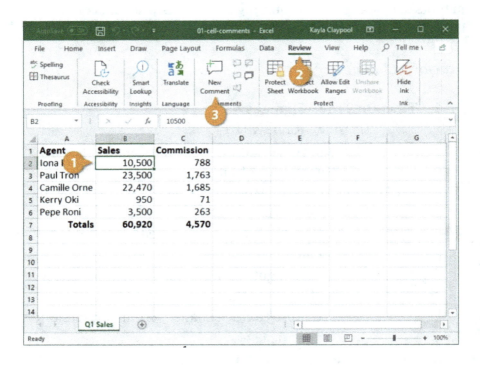

- Type your comment in the text box that appears.

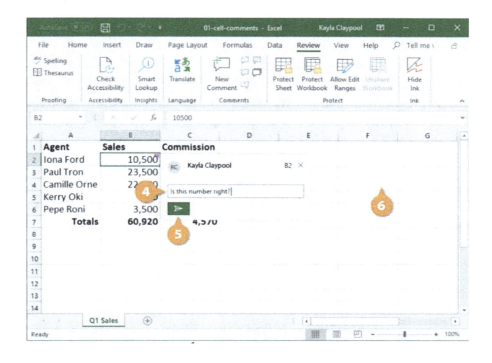

2. **Edit or Delete a Comment**:
   - To edit a comment, right-click the comment box and choose **Edit Comment**.
   - To delete a comment, right-click the comment box and select **Delete Comment**.
3. **Viewing Comments**:
   - Hover over a cell with a comment to view it.
   - Comments are often displayed as small red triangles in the corner of a cell.
4. **Using Threaded Comments**:
   - In more recent versions of Excel, threaded comments allow multiple users to reply to a single comment, making it easier to have discussions directly within the worksheet.

187

Sharing Workbooks Online via OneDrive

Excel integrates seamlessly with OneDrive, Microsoft's cloud storage solution, allowing you to easily share and co-author workbooks online. By saving your workbook to OneDrive, you can collaborate with others in real-time, ensuring that everyone has access to the latest version of the document.

How to Share a Workbook:

1. **Save Your Workbook to OneDrive**:
   o Open your workbook.
   o Click on the **File** tab, then **Save As**, and select **OneDrive** as the save location.
2. **Share the Workbook**:
   o Once the workbook is saved on OneDrive, click the **Share** button in the upper-right corner of the Excel window.
   o You can choose to **invite people by email** or **copy the link** to send directly to collaborators.
3. **Set Permissions**:
   o When sharing, you can specify whether others can **edit** or **view** the document.
   o You can also set an expiration date for access or require a password to open the workbook.

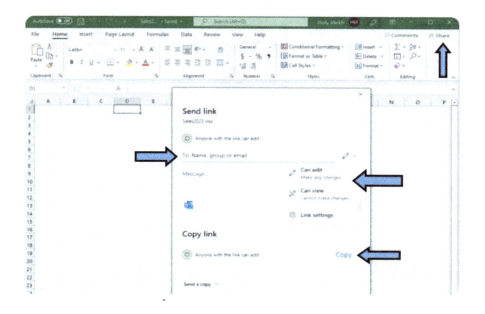

4. **Co-Authoring**:
   - If others are also working on the file, you'll see their names in the upper-right corner of the Excel window.
   - As changes are made, Excel will update the document in real-time, allowing everyone to see edits immediately.

How to Collaborate with OneDrive:

1. **View Changes in Real-Time**:
   - Excel provides a live view of who is editing the document, showing where each user is working on the sheet.
2. **Resolve Conflicts**:
   - If two users make conflicting edits, Excel will alert you to the issue and give you options to resolve it.

3. **Version History**:
   - o OneDrive maintains a version history of your workbook. If needed, you can view or revert to a previous version of the document.
   - o To access this, click **File**, select **Info**, and choose **Version History**.

Pro Tips for Collaboration and Sharing:

- **Use Excel Online**: Excel Online provides many of the same features as the desktop version, but it runs in a web browser, making it easy to collaborate with anyone who has access to the document, no matter where they are.
- **Notify Collaborators**: After sharing a workbook, it's often helpful to send a message or email to your collaborators, letting them know they can access the document and pointing out any important tasks or changes that need attention.
- **Regularly Check for Changes**: If you're working with multiple collaborators, check in frequently to monitor changes and review any feedback or comments.

Chapter 11. Printing and Exporting Worksheets

Printing and exporting worksheets are crucial tasks in Excel when you need to share or present your data outside of the digital environment. Whether you're preparing a hard copy of your report or exporting data to a universally accessible format like PDF, Excel provides a variety of tools to ensure your document prints or exports as expected. In this chapter, we will walk through the process of **setting print areas**, **scaling worksheets**, and **exporting to PDF**.

Setting Print Areas and Page Layouts

Before you print your worksheet, you need to define the areas you want to print and adjust the layout to make sure your data fits neatly on the page.

How to Set a Print Area:

1. **Select the Cells to Print**:
   - Highlight the cells that you want to print. This could be a range of cells, an entire table, or even just specific data that you want to highlight.
2. **Set the Print Area**:
   - Go to the **Page Layout** tab in the Ribbon.
   - Click on **Print Area** in the **Page Setup** group.

- o Choose **Set Print Area**. This will designate the selected cells as the area to print, and only this part of the worksheet will be printed.

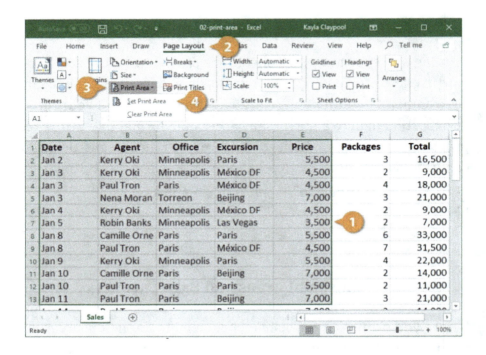

Clearing the Print Area:

If you no longer want to print a specific area, you can clear the print area by following these steps:

1. Go to the **Page Layout** tab.
2. Click on **Print Area**, then select **Clear Print Area**.

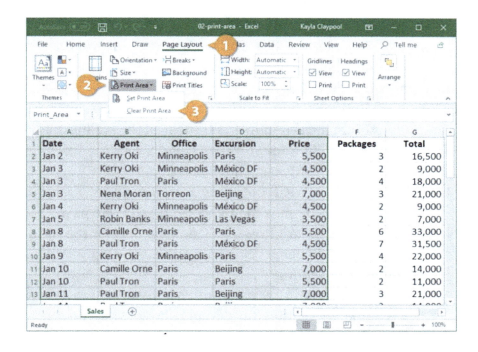

Scaling Worksheets to Fit Pages

Scaling is essential when you need to fit your data into a limited number of pages. Excel allows you to scale your worksheets up or down to fit them on a single page or to spread them across multiple pages. There are several ways to control this:

Automatic Scaling:

Excel provides an automatic scaling option to fit the entire worksheet onto a set number of pages (one page wide, one page tall, etc.).

1. **Go to the File Tab**:
   - o Click on the **File** tab and select **Print** to access the print preview.
2. **Choose Scaling Options**:
   - o Under **Settings**, click on the **No Scaling** dropdown.
   - o From the dropdown, select one of the scaling options:
     - ▪ **Fit Sheet on One Page**: Scales the worksheet to fit everything on a single page.
     - ▪ **Fit All Columns on One Page**: Scales the columns to fit horizontally on one page.
     - ▪ **Fit All Rows on One Page**: Scales the rows to fit vertically on one page.
3. **Preview the Scaling**:
   - o As you adjust scaling options, the print preview will update automatically to show you how your document will look on the page.

Custom Scaling:

For more control over how your data fits on the page, you can manually adjust the scaling by specifying a percentage or setting the width and height of the printed page.

1. **Go to the Page Layout Tab**:
   - o In the **Page Layout** tab, locate the **Scale to Fit** group.
2. **Adjust Scaling**:
   - o Use the **Width** and **Height** dropdowns to choose the number of pages you want the document to fit across.
   - o Alternatively, adjust the **Scale** box to manually set the percentage at which the worksheet will be printed.

Exporting to PDF and Sharing

Exporting your Excel worksheet to a PDF is an excellent way to share data with others while preserving its layout and formatting. Whether you're sending out reports, forms, or workbooks, Excel's export functionality allows you to create professional, shareable documents.

How to Export to PDF:

1. **Go to the File Tab**:
   - Click on the **File** tab and select **Export** from the menu.
2. **Choose Create PDF/XPS Document**:
   - In the Export menu, click **Create PDF/XPS Document**.
3. **Adjust PDF Settings**:
   - In the **Publish as PDF or XPS** dialog box, select the location where you want to save the file and give it a name.
   - Under **Optimize for**, you can select either:
     - **Standard (publishing online and printing)**: Best for high-quality printing.
     - **Minimum size (publishing online)**: Smaller file size for quicker downloads.
4. **Set Additional Options**:
   - If you want to export only a selected portion of your worksheet (such as a print area), click on the **Options** button.

- Choose whether to export the entire workbook, a single sheet, or the current selection.
5. **Save the PDF**:
   - After adjusting any settings, click **Publish** to save the PDF.

Sharing the PDF:

Once you've exported your worksheet as a PDF, you can share it easily via email or upload it to cloud storage for others to download.

1. **Email Directly from Excel**:
   - After exporting the PDF, go to the **File** tab and select **Share**.
   - Choose **Email** to send the document as an attachment directly from Excel.
2. **Upload to Cloud Storage**:
   - You can also upload the PDF to cloud services like **OneDrive** or **Google Drive** to make it easily accessible to others.

Tips for Exporting to PDF:

- **Fit to One Page**: If you're concerned about document size, try adjusting the scaling in Excel before exporting to ensure the data fits properly on a PDF page.
- **Securing PDFs**: After exporting, consider using tools outside of Excel to encrypt or password-protect the PDF file for added security when sharing sensitive data.

Printing Your Excel Worksheet

If you need to produce a hard copy of your Excel worksheet, Excel's print functionality provides several options for customizing the printout to suit your needs.

How to Print:

1. **Go to the File Tab**:
   - Click on the **File** tab and select **Print**.
2. **Select Printer and Settings**:
   - Choose the printer you want to use from the Printer dropdown.
   - Under **Settings**, select the print range (e.g., entire workbook, selection, or active sheet).
   - You can also set other print options like paper size, orientation (portrait or landscape), and margin sizes.
3. **Preview the Printout**:
   - Excel will display a print preview, showing exactly how the document will appear when printed. If necessary, adjust settings like scaling and page breaks before printing.
4. **Click Print**:
   - Once you're satisfied with the preview and settings, click **Print**.

Printing Tips:

- **Print Area**: Make sure you have set the print area before printing to ensure only the necessary data is printed.

- **Multiple Pages**: If the worksheet spans multiple pages, Excel will add page numbers and allow you to control the page breaks to make sure data appears in the right place.

Pro Tips for Printing and Exporting:

- **Print Preview**: Always use the print preview feature before printing to ensure the document will look the way you expect, especially if you have a large worksheet.
- **PDF for Distribution**: Exporting to PDF is an excellent way to distribute your data digitally without worrying about formatting issues on different devices.
- **Printing Selection**: If you only need to print a specific range, select the data you want, and then choose **Print Selection** in the print settings.

Part 3: Integration of Microsoft Word and Excel

Chapter 1. Linking and Embedding Excel Data in Word

Excel and Word are both powerful tools that can work together seamlessly to enhance your documents. Whether you're embedding Excel data directly into a Word document or linking it for automatic updates, you can easily integrate the two applications for more dynamic, data-driven content.

Embedding Excel Tables in Word Documents

Embedding an Excel table into a Word document allows you to display the data as part of the document. This data becomes part of the Word file itself, meaning it's stored within the Word document.

How to Embed Excel Data in Word:

1. **Copy the Excel Data**:
   - In Excel, select the range of cells you want to embed.
   - Right-click and select **Copy**, or press **Ctrl+C**.
2. **Paste the Data in Word**:
   - Open the Word document where you want to insert the data.
   - Go to the location where you want the table to appear.
   - Click on the **Home** tab, then click the **Paste** dropdown.

- o Choose **Paste Special** from the dropdown menu.
3. **Choose Embed Option**:
    - o In the Paste Special dialog box, choose **Microsoft Excel Worksheet Object**.
    - o Click **OK**. The Excel data will now appear embedded in the Word document.
    - o You can double-click the embedded data to open it in Excel for editing. Changes made in Excel will only update when you open the embedded object.

Linking Excel Data to Word for Automatic Updates

Linking Excel data to Word allows you to maintain a live connection between your Excel data and your Word document. This means that whenever the data in Excel is updated, it will automatically reflect in Word.

How to Link Excel Data to Word:

1. **Copy the Excel Data**:
    - o Select the data in Excel that you want to link.
    - o Right-click and select **Copy**, or press **Ctrl+C**.
2. **Paste the Data in Word**:
    - o Open your Word document and place the cursor where you want the data to appear.
    - o Go to the **Home** tab and click the **Paste** dropdown.
    - o Select **Paste Special**.
3. **Choose Link Option**:
    - o In the Paste Special dialog box, select **Paste Link** and choose **Microsoft Excel Worksheet Object**.

- Click **OK**. Now, whenever the data in the linked Excel file is updated, the Word document will reflect those changes automatically.

4. **Update Links**:
   - Word typically prompts you to update linked content when opening the document. You can also manually update links by right-clicking the linked Excel data and selecting **Update Link**.

Chapter 2. Mail Merge with Excel Data

Mail Merge is a powerful tool for creating personalized documents, such as letters or labels, by merging data from an Excel spreadsheet into a Word template. This is useful for sending bulk personalized emails, creating mailing labels, or generating individual letters based on a list of contacts.

Creating Letters and Labels Using Excel as a Data Source

Mail Merge works by using Excel data as a "data source" to populate predefined fields in your Word document template.

Steps to Create Letters Using Excel Data:

1. **Prepare Your Excel Data**:
   - Open Excel and organize the data you want to use in the mail merge, such as names, addresses, or other personalized details. Each column in Excel represents a data field (e.g., First Name, Last Name, Address, etc.).
2. **Set Up Your Word Document**:
   - Open Word and go to the **Mailings** tab.
   - Click **Start Mail Merge** and select the type of document you want to create (e.g., **Letters**).
3. **Select Recipients**:
   - Click **Select Recipients** and choose **Use an Existing List**.

- Browse to select the Excel file that contains your data and click **Open**.

4. **Insert Merge Fields**:
   - Place your cursor where you want to insert personalized information in the Word document (e.g., name, address).
   - Click **Insert Merge Field** and select the corresponding column from your Excel file (e.g., First Name, Last Name).

5. **Preview and Complete the Merge**:
   - Click **Preview Results** to see how the merged data will look in your document.
   - If everything looks correct, click **Finish & Merge** to print or send the personalized letters.

Steps to Create Mailing Labels Using Excel Data:

- Follow the same process as creating letters, but select **Labels** from the **Start Mail Merge** menu.
- In the label options, choose your preferred label format (e.g., Avery).
- Insert merge fields for the name and address, then complete the merge to generate the labels.

Chapter 3. Using Word and Excel Together for Reports

Combining Word's powerful formatting and layout tools with Excel's data analysis capabilities makes it easier to create professional reports. You can insert Excel tables, charts, and pivot tables into Word for a comprehensive document that includes both detailed data and formatted text.

Combining Word's Formatting Features with Excel's Data Analysis

Here's how to integrate the two programs effectively:

1. **Incorporating Excel Data into Word**:
   o **Tables**: As discussed earlier, you can embed or link Excel tables into Word to display your data in a structured format.
   o **Charts**: You can create a chart in Excel, copy it, and paste it into Word. You can also embed it so it remains editable or link it for automatic updates.
2. **Creating Interactive Reports**:
   o Use **Excel PivotTables** for data analysis and summarize your findings. Then, copy and paste the PivotTable into your Word report for a clear, concise summary.

- o Use **Excel Formulas and Functions** to analyze your data and create meaningful insights, then export the data into Word for a polished final report.
3. **Formatting the Document**:
   - o Use Word's styling tools to format your text and structure your report. You can apply headings, bullet points, numbered lists, and more to make the document easier to read.
   - o Combine this with Excel's visual elements (charts, tables) for a professional, data-driven report.
4. **Automating Report Creation**:
   - o By linking Excel data to your Word report, you can automatically generate updated reports with new data without manually editing the document each time.

Pro Tips for Using Word and Excel Together:

- **Update Links**: When linking Excel data to Word, be sure to update the links before finalizing the document to ensure the most up-to-date data is displayed.
- **Protect Excel Data**: When embedding or linking Excel data in Word, consider protecting the Excel file if it contains sensitive information.
- **Formatting Consistency**: To ensure a professional report, keep the formatting consistent across Word and Excel, such as font styles, colors, and header sizes.

Part 4: Appendices and Additional Resources

1. Microsoft Word Cheat Sheet

Here's a quick reference to some of the most commonly used shortcuts and tips in Microsoft Word to help boost productivity:

Common Shortcuts for Productivity:

- **Ctrl + N**: New document
- **Ctrl + O**: Open document
- **Ctrl + S**: Save document
- **Ctrl + P**: Print document
- **Ctrl + C**: Copy selected text
- **Ctrl + X**: Cut selected text
- **Ctrl + V**: Paste copied/cut text
- **Ctrl + Z**: Undo the last action
- **Ctrl + Y**: Redo the last undone action
- **Ctrl + B**: Bold text
- **Ctrl + I**: Italicize text
- **Ctrl + U**: Underline text
- **Ctrl + L**: Align text to the left
- **Ctrl + E**: Center-align text
- **Ctrl + R**: Right-align text
- **Ctrl + J**: Justify text
- **Ctrl + A**: Select all text
- **Ctrl + F**: Find text
- **Ctrl + H**: Replace text
- **Ctrl + K**: Insert hyperlink
- **Ctrl + T**: Create a hanging indent
- **Ctrl + Shift + N**: Apply the Normal style

Productivity Tips:

- **Format Painter**: Use the Format Painter (found in the Home tab) to copy formatting from one part of your document to another.
- **Navigation Pane**: Use **Ctrl + F** to open the Navigation pane for quick jumping between sections.
- **Headers and Footers**: Use these for consistent information, such as page numbers, document title, or author's name.
- **Track Changes**: Use the **Review** tab to track changes and collaborate on documents.
- **Keyboard Shortcuts for Styles**: Use **Alt + Ctrl + 1, Alt + Ctrl + 2**, etc., to quickly apply styles like Heading 1, Heading 2, etc.

---

2. Microsoft Excel Cheat Sheet

Excel is loaded with useful formulas, functions, and shortcuts that make data management efficient. Here's a cheat sheet to help you navigate through them:

Common Formulas and Functions:

- **SUM(range)**: Adds up all numbers in the specified range.
- **AVERAGE(range)**: Calculates the average of the numbers in the specified range.
- **COUNT(range)**: Counts the number of cells in the range that contain numbers.
- **MAX(range)**: Returns the largest value in the specified range.

- **MIN(range)**: Returns the smallest value in the specified range.
- **IF(logical_test, value_if_true, value_if_false)**: Conditional logic function.
- **VLOOKUP(lookup_value, table_array, col_index_num, [range_lookup])**: Looks up a value in the first column of a range and returns a value in the same row from another column.
- **HLOOKUP(lookup_value, table_array, row_index_num, [range_lookup])**: Similar to VLOOKUP, but searches for a value in the top row of a table.
- **SUMIF(range, criteria, [sum_range])**: Adds numbers in a range that meet specific criteria.
- **COUNTIF(range, criteria)**: Counts cells in a range that meet a specified condition.
- **CONCATENATE(text1, text2, ...)** or **&**: Combines multiple text strings into one.
- **TEXT(value, format_text)**: Converts a number into a text in a specified format (e.g., **TEXT(12345, "$#,##0")**).

Common Shortcuts:

- **Ctrl + N**: New workbook
- **Ctrl + O**: Open workbook
- **Ctrl + S**: Save workbook
- **Ctrl + P**: Print workbook
- **Ctrl + C**: Copy selection
- **Ctrl + X**: Cut selection
- **Ctrl + V**: Paste copied/cut content
- **Ctrl + Z**: Undo action
- **Ctrl + Y**: Redo action

- **Ctrl + F**: Find
- **Ctrl + H**: Find and replace
- **Ctrl + A**: Select all
- **Ctrl + Shift + L**: Add or remove filters
- **Ctrl + Shift + "+"**: Insert a new row or column
- **Alt + E, S, V**: Paste special (useful for formulas, values, or formatting)

---

3. Glossary of Terms

Microsoft Word and Excel Terminology:

- **Cell**: A single data entry box in Excel, defined by a row and column intersection.
- **Workbook**: A file that contains one or more worksheets (in Excel).
- **Worksheet**: A single sheet within a workbook (in Excel).
- **PivotTable**: A data summarization tool used in Excel to automatically sort, count, and total data.
- **Formula**: A calculation used in Excel to perform mathematical or logical operations.
- **Range**: A selection of two or more cells in Excel.
- **Cell Reference**: The address of a cell, such as **A1**, which denotes the cell in the first column and first row.
- **Function**: A predefined formula in Excel (e.g., **SUM, AVERAGE**).
- **Table**: A structured data set in Excel that is organized into rows and columns.

4. Practice Projects

Word Practice Projects:

- **Create a Resume**: Use Word's templates or design a custom resume with different sections, formatting, and styling.
- **Design a Flyer**: Create a promotional flyer by inserting images, adding text, and using various formatting tools.
- **Write a Report**: Compile a report with headings, subheadings, bullet points, and charts. Use proper formatting and apply a table of contents.

Excel Practice Projects:

- **Build a Budget**: Create a personal or business budget using Excel's cell references and basic functions like **SUM** and **IF** to track income and expenses.
- **Create a Simple Invoice**: Design a simple invoice template where you can input customer information, item details, and calculate totals.
- **Analyze Sales Data**: Import or input sales data into Excel, then use PivotTables, functions like **SUMIF** and **COUNTIF**, and charts to analyze performance.

5. Troubleshooting and FAQ

Common Issues and Solutions:

- **Problem: Excel Formulas Not Calculating**
  Solution: Check that the formula has been entered correctly. Make sure the **Calculation Option** is set to **Automatic** (under **Formulas** tab > **Calculation Options**).
- **Problem: Word Freezing or Crashing**
  Solution: Try restarting Word, or use **Ctrl + Shift + Esc** to open the Task Manager and end any unresponsive processes. Consider disabling add-ins if the issue persists.
- **Problem: Cells Not Aligning Properly in Excel**
  Solution: Adjust the cell alignment using the alignment options under the **Home** tab. You may also need to adjust row height or column width to fit the content.
- **Problem: Page Numbers in Word Not Starting from 1**
  Solution: Insert a **Section Break** before the page where you want the numbering to start. Then, go to **Insert** > **Page Numbers** and choose **Format Page Numbers** to set the starting number.
- **Problem: Excel Not Responding to Keyboard Shortcuts**
  Solution: Ensure the **Num Lock** and **Scroll Lock** keys are set correctly. Also, check if the keyboard shortcuts are disabled by an add-in or system settings.

Index

www.ingramcontent.com/pod-product-compliance
Lightning Source LLC
LaVergne TN
LVHW012334060326
832902LV00012B/1882